THE POSSIBILITY
OF AN ABSOLUTE ARCHITECTURE

Writing **Architecture** series
A project of the Anyone Corporation; Cynthia Davidson, editor

Earth Moves: The Furnishing of Territories
Bernard Cache, 1995

Architecture as Metaphor: Language, Number, Money
Kojin Karatani, 1995

Differences: Topographies of Contemporary Architecture
Ignasi de Solà-Morales, 1996

Constructions
John Rajchman, 1997

Such Places as Memory
John Hejduk, 1998

Welcome to The Hotel Architecture
Roger Connah, 1998

Fire and Memory: On Architecture and Energy
Luis Fernández-Galiano, 2000

A Landscape of Events
Paul Virilio, 2000

Architecture from the Outside: Essays on Virtual and Real Space
Elizabeth Grosz, 2001

Public Intimacy: Architecture and the Visual Arts
Giuliana Bruno, 2007

Strange Details
Michael Cadwell, 2007

Histories of the Immediate Present: Inventing Architectural Modernism
Anthony Vidler, 2008

Drawing for Architecture
Leon Krier, 2009

Architecture's Desire: Reading the Late Avant-Garde
K. Michael Hays, 2010

The Possibility of an Absolute Architecture
Pier Vittorio Aureli, 2011

The Alphabet and the Algorithm
Mario Carpo, 2011

THE MIT PRESS

CAMBRIDGE, MASSACHUSETTS

LONDON, ENGLAND

THE POSSIBILITY
OF AN ABSOLUTE ARCHITECTURE

PIER VITTORIO AURELI

MIT Press books may be purchased at special quantity discounts for business or sales promotional use. For information, please email special_sales@mitpress.mit.edu.

This book was set in Filosofia and Trade Gothic by the MIT Press. Printed and bound in the United States of America.

Library of Congress Cataloging-in-Publication Data

Aureli, Pier Vittorio.
The possibility of an absolute architecture / Pier Vittorio Aureli.
p. cm. — (Writing architecture)
Includes bibliographical references and index.
ISBN 978-0-262-51579-5 (pbk. : alk. paper)
1. Architecture. 2. Cities and towns. I. Title.
NA2540.A97 2011
720.1—dc22

2010030741

10   9   8   7   6   5   4   3

CONTENTS

ACKNOWLEDGMENTS

I offer deep thanks to Cynthia Davidson for her continuous support, critical help, and editorial work on the manuscript of this book. Without her strong encouragement and patience the book would not exist. Thanks also to Matthew Abbate and the MIT Press.

The following people have been important in shaping the content of the book in different ways, consciously or unconsciously: Wiel Arets, Marco Biraghi, Cesare Birignani, Alice Bulla, Luca Galofaro, Maria Shéhérazade Giudici, Elias Guenoun, Ariane Lourie Harrison, Rolf Jenni, Gabriele Mastrigli, Vedran Mimica, Philippe Morell, Joan Ockman, Manuel Orazi, Bernardo Secchi, Lukasz Stanek, Brett Steele, Roemer van Toorn, Thomas Weaver, Alejandro Zaera Polo, and Guido Zuliani. The Berlage Institute in Rotterdam and the Architectural Association in London have been welcoming platforms for the development of the ideas expressed in this book. Fundamental discussions with Umberto Barbieri, Andrea Branzi, Peter Eisenman, Gabriele Mastrigli, Martino Tattara, Mario Tronti, and Elia Zenghelis have directly influenced the writing.

I dedicate this book to my parents and my sister.

INTRODUCTION

This book proposes to reconsider architectural form in light of a unitary interpretation of architecture and the city. This unitary interpretation is put forward via the paradox of a unilateral synthesis: a unitary interpretation made from *within* projects on architectural form itself. This unilateral synthesis addresses the possibility of interpreting architectural form as the index for the constitution of an idea of the city. In order to highlight the constitutive paradox implied in such a thesis, I have defined the object of this book as absolute architecture.

The term *absolute* is intended to stress, as much as possible, the individuality of the architectural form when this form is confronted with the environment in which it is conceived and constructed. I use *absolute* not in the conventional sense of "purity" but in its original meaning as something being resolutely itself after being "separated" from its other.[1] In the pursuit of the possibility of an absolute architecture, the other is the space of the city, its extensive organization, and its government.

In the course of history, certain architects have articulated the autonomy of form through a radical and systematic confrontation with the city in which they have operated. If politics is agonism through separation and confrontation, it is precisely in the process of separation inherent in the making of architectural form that the political in architecture lies, and thus the possibility of understanding the agonistic relationship between architecture and its context. The very condition of architectural form is to separate and to be separated. Through its act of separation and being separated, architecture reveals *at once* the essence of the city and the essence of itself as political form: the city as the composition of (separate) parts.

In the first chapter, I theorize the possibility of an absolute architecture by introducing the categories of the formal and the political in architecture. The formal and the political are overlapping categories, as they both address the possibility of separation, composition, and counterposition; in architecture, these categories are interpreted within the separateness implied in the constitution of architectural form. For this reason the formal and the political are seen as the basis not only of architectural form, but also of the idea of the city. Both the idea of architecture and the idea of the city as defined through the categories of the formal and the political are mobilized against the ethos of urbanization, the "managerial" paradigm that, within the rise of capitalism, has characterized our global civilization since the twilight of the so-called Middle Ages. Urbanization is here understood according to Ildefons Cerdà's initial use of the term as the ever-expanding and all-encompassing apparatus that is at the basis of modern forms of governance. These modern forms of governance consist in the absorption of the political dimension of coexistence (the city) within the economic logic of social management (urbanization).

It is precisely within the rise of the space of urbanization that architecture as the project of the finite, and thus separated, form(s) can be read as critical, inasmuch as it both obeys the managerial principle of urbanization and its extensive logic of total integration, yet makes explicit and tangible the inexorable separateness of the city, since the city is made not only of flows but also of stoppages, walls, boundaries, and partitions. Of course, urbanization is not an apparatus made of flows; it is made of closures and of strategic forms of containment. Today it is clear that the outcome of the logic of urban governance manifests itself not only in the smooth space of global economic transactions, but also, and especially, in the proliferation of enclaves, walls, and apparatuses of control and closure established in order to maintain the "smoothness" of global economic trade. This is nothing new. The rise of urbanization as an apparatus of governance is marked precisely by the constant dialectic of integration and closure. Within urbanization, integration and closure are not the consequence of each other, but are two simultaneous phenomena meant to reinforce each other. The possibility of an absolute architecture consists in the alteration of this dialectic by reclaiming separation, not only as part of the principle of urban management but as a form that exceeds it. In this way the possibility of an absolute architecture is the attempt to reestablish the sense of the city as the site of a political confrontation and recomposition of parts. While the urban theories of Cerdà, Ludwig Hilberseimer, Archizoom, and Rem Koolhaas are seen here as the most extreme paradigmatic projects of urbanization, the late work of Ludwig Mies van der Rohe is interpreted as demonstrating the possibility of an absolute architecture. Mies's late projects absorbed the reifying forces of urbanization, but presented them not as ubiquitous but as finite, clearly separated parts.

The idea of separated parts links the possibility of an absolute architecture to the idea of the archipelago as a form for the city. The concept of the archipelago describes a condition where parts are separated yet united by the common ground of their juxtaposition. In contrast to the integrative apparatus of urbanization, the archipelago envisions the city as the agonistic struggle of parts whose forms are finite and yet, by virtue of their finiteness, are in constant relationship both with each other and with the "sea" that frames and delimits them. The islands of the archipelago describe the role of architectural form within a space more and more dominated by the "sea" of urbanization. The islands are framed by this sea, yet their formal boundaries allow them to be understood as what frames and, to a certain extent, (re)defines the sea between the islands. Such an act of framing and redefinition consists not in the imposition of a general principle or of an overall norm, but in the strategic deployment of specific architectural forms that act as frames, and thus as a limit to urbanization. These forms are the opposite of what today are called "iconic buildings." Iconic buildings are typically singular landmarks whose agency is inscribed entirely within the logic of urbanization. Indeed, the agenda of the iconic building is a postpolitical architecture stripped bare of any meaning other than the celebration of corporate economic performance. In this sense, rather than being agonistic forms, contemporary "icons" are the final and celebratory manifestations of the *Grundnorm* of urbanization: the victory of economic optimization over political judgment. The islands of the archipelago, on the other hand, confront the forces of urbanization by opposing to urbanization's ubiquitous power their explicitness as forms, as punctual, circumscribed facts, as stoppages.

This understanding of architecture was the trigger for my revisiting the work of four architects whose project was advanced through the making of architectural form, but whose concern was the city at large. Using the metaform of the archipelago, I attempt to identify the project of the city in the work advanced by Andrea Palladio, Giovanni Battista Piranesi, Étienne-Louis Boullée, and Oswald Mathias Ungers. On the one hand, the choice of these architects is subjective and motivated by my profound interest in their work, which I have approached not as a historian but as an architect interested in the work of other architects. At the same time, the work of these architects addressed the transformations of the modern city and its urban implications not through a general vision for the city, but through the elaboration of specific and strategic architectural forms. For this reason, their respective projects for the city do not take the form of an overall plan but are manifested as an archipelago of site-specific interventions. The themes and concepts that frame these interventions can be seen as the stepping-stones of a strategy, and thus of a project, that attempts to reinvent the city. Consequently, this book does not argue for the autonomy of design, but rather for the *autonomy of the project*, for the possibility of architectural thought to propose an alternative idea of the city rather than simply confirming its existing conditions. The difference between the idea of the project and the idea of design is crucial here. Design reflects the mere managerial praxis of building something, whereas the project indicates the *strategy* on whose basis something must be produced, must be brought into presence. In the idea of the project, the strategy exceeds the mere act of building and acquires a meaning in itself: an act of decision and judgment on the reality that the design or building of something addresses.

For this reason, the forms advanced by these four architects are described in terms of how their themes and concepts have resonated with the political, social, and cultural circumstances of each city. In each case I emphasize how the project of a specific architectural form is at once an act of radical autonomy from and radical engagement with the forces that characterized the urbanization of cities.

Apart from Ungers, none of the architects discussed here ever presented his projects in terms of an archipelago. Representing their work within the idea of the city as an archipelago is precisely the argument of this book. The asymmetry between the scale of architectural form and the overwhelming vastness of the urban scale provoked these architects to elaborate architectural form toward the possibility of being not a general rule but an example for the city. In this way, each architectural intervention is bound to a conceptual continuity that transforms the episodic nature of each intervention (built or unbuilt) into islands of the archipel-ago: the general project of the city that manifests itself through the exceptional and "insular" form of architecture. The possibil-ity of an absolute architecture is thus both the possibility of *mak-ing* the city and also the possibility of *understanding* the city and its opposing force—urbanization—through the very finite nature of architectural form.

1 TOWARD THE ARCHIPELAGO
DEFINING THE POLITICAL AND THE FORMAL IN ARCHITECTURE

If white and black blend, soften, and unite
A thousand ways, is there no black or white?
—Alexander Pope, *Essay on Man*, 1733

Architecture has been popular in recent years. Ironically, how-ever, its growing popularity is inversely proportional to the increasing sense of political powerlessness and cultural disillu-sionment many architects feel about their effective contribution to the built world. Within this paradoxical situation—and beyond the phenomenon of architecture's "success"—it is necessary to face and acknowledge the popularity of architecture critically. To do so, we need to seriously address the unequivocal social and cultural power architecture possesses to produce represen-tations of the world through exemplary forms of built reality. At this level, the problem of *form*—that is, the strategizing of ar-chitecture's being—becomes crucial. The making of form is thus the real and effective necessary program of architecture.

But what form can architecture define within the contempo-rary city without falling into the current self-absorbed perfor-mances of iconic buildings, parametric designs, or redundant mappings of every possible complexity and contradiction of the urban world? What sort of significant and critical relationship can architecture aspire to in a world that is no longer constituted by the idea and the motivations of the city, but is instead dominated by urbanization? In what follows I will attempt to reconstruct the possibility of an architecture of the city that is no longer situated only in the autonomous realm of its disciplinary status, but must directly confront urbanization. This possibility is put forward in two ways: first, by critically understanding the essential difference between the concept of the city and the concept of urbanization—how these concepts overlap, as well as how they address two radically different interpretations of inhabited space—and second, by looking at how urbanization has historically come to prevail over the city. I will show the rise of urbanization not through its presumed "real" effects, but through exemplary projects for cities, which here are understood as effective representations not simply of urbanization itself but also of its logic. In an argument critical of the logic of urbanization (and its instigator, capitalism), I will redefine *political* and *formal* as concepts that can define architecture's essence as form. Finally, using these concepts as a springboard, I will illustrate a counterproject for the city—the archipelago—by referring to a specific architectural form that is a counterform within and against the totality of urbanization. This project will lead to what I see as a preliminary introduction for a definition of architecture itself, or what I define as the possibility of an absolute architecture.

Polis, Civitas, Urbs

Aristotle made a fundamental distinction between politics and economics—the distinction between what he defines as *technè politikè* and *technè oikonomikè*.[1] What he calls *technè politikè* is the faculty of decision making for the sake of the public interest—decision making for the common good, for the way individuals and different groups of people can live together. Politics in this sense comes from the existence of the *polis*[2] (and not the other way around). The *polis* is the space of the many, the space that exists *in between* individuals or groups of individuals when they coexist. However, contrary to Aristotle, who assumed that "man is a political animal" by nature, and thus conceived of the institution of politics as natural, we can say that political space—the space in between—is not a natural or given phenomena. Political space is made into the institution of politics precisely because the existence of the space in between presupposes potential conflict among the parts that form it. This possibility is the very foundation of *technè politikè*—the art of politics—the decision making that must turn conflict into coexistence (albeit without eradicating the possibility of conflict). Precisely because politics is incarnated in the *polis*—the project of the city—the existence of the *polis* holds the possibility of conflict and the need for its resolution as its very ontological foundation.

Technè oikonomikè—economy—concerns the administration of private space par excellence: the house, or *oikos*, from which the word *oikonomikè* derives. Aristotle's *oikos* is a complex organism of relationships that he divides into three categories: despotic relationships, such as master-slave; paternal relationships, such as parent to child; and marriage relationships, such as husband to wife. Unlike political space, in the space of *oikos*, human relationships are given, unchangeable, and despotic (for Aristotle, the despot is the subject who governs the *oikos*). *Oikonomikè* concerns the wise administration of the house and control over the relationships of its members. The principle of economy can be distinguished from the principle of politics in the same way that the house is distinguished from the *polis*. Unlike politics, the authority of economy acts not in the public interest but in its own interest; furthermore, it cannot be questioned because its sphere is not the pubic space of the *polis* but the private space of the house. This distinction originated in the Greek city-state, where there was a contrast between two constituent elements: the *oikoi*—the agglomeration of houses—and the political space of the agora, where opinions are exchanged and public decisions are made. The private space of the house is the basic social space that ensures the natural reproduction of its members; the public space of the agora is the political space where discussion and confrontation for the sake of the public interest takes place. The history of cities in the West can be summarized in this at times latent and ambiguous, at times evident struggle between public and private interests, between political interests and economic interests. In the Roman city, an analogous struggle played itself out in the dichotomy between *urbs* and *civitas*. The Latin term *urbs* indicated "city" in a different sense from the Greek word *polis*. The term *urbs* addressed the very material constitution of the city. In principle, an *urbs* was a walled agglomeration of houses without further political qualification.[3] Whereas the *polis* was founded from a preexisting, latent community, the formation of the *urbs* transcended any community, and thus could be founded *ex novo*, in a tabula rasa condition, like the building of a domestic space. From this we can affirm that *urbs* describes a generic condition of protected cohabitation reducible to the principle of the house and its material necessities. While the Greek *polis* was a city strictly framed by its walled perimeter, the Roman *urbs* was not intended to be restricted, and in fact it expanded in the form of a territorial organization, in which roads played a crucial role.

As Hannah Arendt has remarked, the idea of *nomos* (law) was crucial for the ancient Greeks. *Nomos* is law that, rather than regulating political action, frames it within a defined spatial form that coincides with the walled perimeter of the city and the distinction between public and private space.[4] *Nomos* was seen as a frame, as a necessary precondition for politics, but not as an object of politics. The aim of *nomos* was to contain or, better, to counter the infinite nature of relationships that originate from the political life of a *polis*—the "insatiability" that Arendt (following Aeschylus) defines as the inevitable collateral effect of politics, "which can be held in check only by *nomos*, by law in the Greek sense of the word."[5] Arendt writes, "The *nomos* limits actions and prevents them from dissipating into an unforeseeable, constantly expanding system of relationships, and by doing so gives actions their enduring forms, turning each action into a deed that in its greatness—that is, in its surpassing excellence— can be remembered and preserved."[6]

In contrast to the Greek concept of *nomos*, the Roman concept of law, *lex*, was *tout court* a political thing in itself; it required a political consensus of the parties involved in its jurisdiction and its function as a treaty. Unlike the Greek *nomos*, which was a predetermined form that framed the unfolding of political life, the Roman law was a political instrument at the service of Rome's expansionist logic, through which the Romans could force alien populations to be part of an ever-inclusive alliance for the sake of Rome itself.[7] While the *nomos*, by forming a limit, prevented the Greek *polis* from unfolding into a totality, it was precisely the inclusive concept of the *lex* that turned Rome from a *polis* into a *civitas*, and thus into an empire. For this reason the idea of the Greek *polis* can be described as an archipelago, not only because it took this geographical form, but also because the condition of insularity as a mode of relationships was its essential political form.[8] The Roman Empire, by contrast, can be described as an insatiable network in which the empire's diversity became an all-inclusive totality. This totality was the settlement process that originated in the logic of the *urbs*. The *urbs*, in contrast to the insular logic of the Greek *polis*, represents the expansionist and inclusive logic of the Roman territories.[9] The Romans used the term *urbs* to designate the idea of Rome because, in their expansionist logic, Rome was the universal symbolic template for the whole inhabited space of the empire. Thus *urbs* came to designate a universal and generic condition of cohabitation, which is why, as we will see later, it was used by the "inventor" of urbanism, Ildefons Cerdà, to replace the term *ciudad*, which he found too restrictive because it referred to "city"—to the political and symbolic condition of *civitas*.[10]

Within *urbs* is the Roman *civitas*, the condition of citizenship or right to citizenship. Unlike *urbs*, *civitas* concerns not the materiality of inhabited space but the political status of its inhabitants. *Civitas* comes from *cives*,[11] a gathering of people from different origins who decide to coexist under the same law, which in turn gives them the condition of citizenship. As with *urbs*, there is a fundamental difference between the Roman *civitas* and the Greek *polis*. The *civitas* is a gathering of people of different origins, while the Greek *polis* is a community of people who come from the same place (foreigners did not have the right to participate in the political life of the *polis*). However, we can say that both the *polis* and the *civitas* are explicitly political forms of coexistence, unlike the sphere of the *oikos* or, at a different scale, the *urbs*, which indicates the material condition of cohabitation independent of any political sense. By designating the built structure of the city and its functioning without any initial political qualification, the *urbs* can be interpreted as simply the generic aggregation of people—families or clans—and their necessary circulation systems. The form of this aggregation is a "cohabitation," which means that what is shared is simply the material condition of inhabiting a place.

The *civitas* is the gathering of free individuals who come together by recognizing and sharing a public sphere, the existence of which makes them citizens. One can speculate that the Roman *civitas* and *urbs* play complementary roles similar to *technè politikè* and *technè oikonomikè*—of *polis* and *oikos*. But while the *oikos* simply indicates the realm of domestic cohabitation, the *urbs* extends this realm to the structure intended to support the simple aggregation of houses. This structure lies in the space *infra*, or in between them: it is *infrastructure*. If the *infra*, as defined by politics, is a trace of the impetus toward separation and confrontation within the city, the *infra* of the *urbs* is the space of connection and integration. *Urbs* is infrastructure, the network that, starting from the reality and necessity of the habitat, unfolds and aggregates the house within an organic whole that bypasses any political space. Its primary purpose is the functioning of the private space of the family, which it connects to the infrastructure. In the Roman city, *urbs* and *civitas* indicated two irreducible but complementary domains of human association, but these began to overlap and coexist within the same context. Hence, the Roman city manifests what will be the ongoing central dilemma of the city as such. First is the demand for the good *functioning* of the city as a place for cohabitation through its economic administration and the physical manifestation of administration, its urban plan—the *urbs*—without which the city would be an uncomfortable and insecure place. Second is the demand for discussion and confrontation, its political life—*civitas*—without which the city would be the unfolding of a predictable and despotic order of things. The attempt to meet these demands via a single totality has been the deep source of totalitarianism in the real sense of the word—to rule human associations according to one total system that does not differentiate between public and private aspects of human behavior. However, with the rebirth of the Western city after the dissolution of Roman civilization, the distinction between *urbs* and *civitas* was not simply dissolved; rather, the economic impetus of *urbs* gradually took over the political idea of *civitas*.

Unlike the Greek *polis* or the Roman *civitas*, the origins of which were essentially political, the rebirth of the Western city at the turn of the first millennium was propelled primarily by the role of economics: agricultural improvements, the rise of artisanal industry, and the consequent demographic expansion, which created a totally new way of living and working.[12] Though this new form took place within a rural and feudal order, its premises were couched in a fundamental network of economic transactions. The gradual rise of the bourgeoisie, a new social entity that identified with the primary role assumed by the economy, defined (and still defines) the very identity of the contemporary city. The bourgeoisie constituted a new public sphere, one that was no longer *civitas* but rather comprised the interests of owners of private property, who constituted a new form of "public interest." This new form of public interest, however, is paradoxical. It is essentially private because it is in the economic interest of only one segment of the entire social body;[13] but it is also de facto public, because it concerns the primary source of the function of the modern city and modern state: the exchange of commodities and the social domain of work, which is precisely what *urbs* is now meant to support and expand. Colonial urbanism in the Americas, for example, was the ideal projection of this new order. Not by chance, the Laws of the Indies that regulated the layout of new cities in the American colonies were derived from Alberti's precepts in *De re aedificatoria*.[14] In the "New World," as in the colonies of the Roman Empire, the economic efficiency of urbanization was propelled by the military logic of settlement. With the crisis of the ancien régime, the advent of industrialization, and the rise of capitalism, the role of the *urbs* absorbed the idea of *civitas* to the point that over the last three centuries we have witnessed the triumph of a new form of human association based entirely on the mastery of the *urbs*. Enter urbanization.

The word *urbanization* was introduced by the Spanish engineer and planner Ildefons Cerdà, who theorized the concept in his 1867 book *Teoría general de la urbanización*.[15] Conscious of the extreme importance of the phenomena he wanted to describe,[16] Cerdà legitimized his invention of *urbanization* as elucidating the emerging "conceptual" features of a paradigm. This paradigm was the condition of limitlessness and the complete integration of movement and communication brought about by capitalism, which Cerdà saw as the unprecedented "vast swirling ocean of persons, of things, of interests of every sort, of a thousand diverse elements"[17] that work in permanent reciprocity and thus form a totality that cannot be contained by any previous finite territorial formations such as the city. Precisely for this reason, after a careful investigation of the origin of the words available for describing this new condition, he coined the word *urbanization*, deriving it from the word *urbs*, with the intention to replace the word *ciudad* (city), which he found too conditioned by its meaning as *civitas*:

> Since the genuine sense of urbs referred principally to the material part of the grouping of buildings, for all matters referring to the inhabitants [the Romans] used the word civis (citizen), from which they derived all the terms intended to express things, objects, happenstance, and qualities concerning dwellers. The word urbanus (from urbe) referred to matters concerning the material organization of the urbs: so it was that the citizens never called themselves urban, because the root word did not allow for such an application.[18]

Therefore, for Cerdà, the center of the new forms of human habitat was not the city center with its monuments and symbolic spaces, but what lay beyond it: the suburbs.[19] Composed only of roads and individual dwellings, the suburbs, according to Cerdà, offered the best living conditions, and thus the task of urbanization was to expand infrastructure as much as possible in order to develop human habitats beyond the symbolic frame of the city. "To ruralize the city and to urbanize the countryside"[20] was, for Cerdà, the double agenda of urbanization.

The General Theory of Urbanization was written a posteriori in support of Cerdà's proposal to expand the city of Barcelona,[21] which is widely considered the first city plan in history to make systematic use of scientific criteria such as statistics.[22] These criteria were aimed at the homogeneous and controllable redistribution of social wealth, and made clear at the scale of urban design a method of governance in which social wealth and economic control of the working class—and thus the security of urban space—were at stake.[23] For this Cerdà drafted an isotropic grid of 133-by-133-meter blocks, which articulated the equal distribution of services and roads throughout the city area. A religious center appeared in every nine-block district, a marketplace every four blocks, a park every eight, a hospital every sixteen. These were distributed according to a density of 250 inhabitants per hectare, the standard recommended to guarantee a maximum hygienic social order. From the evidence of this careful process of design, where both the geometry of the grid and the conception of urban space as a problem of economic organization were crucial, one can argue that Cerdà's political aim was to avoid class conflict by balancing class differences.[24] However, while his concept of urbanization is indebted to the *damero*, the chessboard grid of colonial cities, it is better understood as a Copernican revolution in the way human habitat is conceived: not as framed within the ideological and historical concept of the city as a centrality, but as a potentially infinite space that extends beyond the centers of cities according to the technological and economic capabilities of a productive society.

Cerdà's grid, conceived as potentially infinite, was to occupy the empty area between old Barcelona and the towns on its outskirts, thereby creating a newly built sea of urban infrastructure linking once separate centers. Quite different from Baron Haussmann's brutal, axis-cutting principle of post-1848 Paris, Cerdà's scientific method distributed services that, in his reformist strategy, would link upgraded working-class living conditions with their social control. As exemplified in Cerdà's plan for Barcelona, urbanization has no representative or iconic function. It is simply a device—it *is* what it *does*: it creates the best conditions for the reproduction of the labor force.

Françoise Choay has argued that what characterizes Cerdà's urbanization is its scientific tone.[25] His implicit invention was to attribute the governance of the city to a process of technological evolution, which is scientific in terms of its productive applicability. Technological development and governance become synonymous in an approach that prioritizes the compatibility of human existence, economic growth, and social security. Urbanization indissolubly and structurally links the motivations for upgrading human life in the urban environment to the possibility of enabling a fertile ground for the reproduction of the labor force and its control, or *governance*. Implicit in Cerdà's idea of urbanization is the suppression of the city's political character in favor of a form of power that Giorgio Agamben has defined as a "paradigma gestionale" (a managerial paradigm)—economy in its original sense as the administration of the house.[26] One can argue that the notion of urbanization presupposes the fundamental substitution of politics with economics as a mode of city governance to the point that today it is reasonable—almost

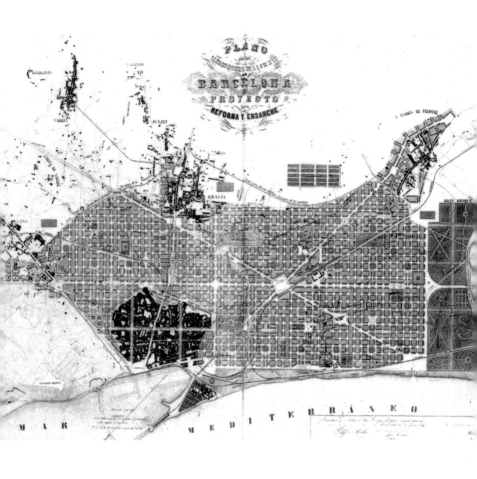

1.1
Ildefons Cerdà, Plan for Barcelona, 1860.
Urbanization replaces the city. Following colonial
cities in the Americas, Cerdà's plan for Barcelona
exemplified the role of urbanization as the new
form of biopolitical government. The result is a plan
that optimizes urban infrastructure.

banal—to ask not what kind of political power is governing us, but whether we are governed by politics at all—that is, whether we are living under a totalitarian managerial process based on economy, which in turn uses different political modes of public governance ranging from dictatorship to democracy to war. Of course an economy acts politically, but its politics ultimately aims to establish economic criteria as the primary organization of the human environment. At the center of this principle, from Cerdà on, the fundamental space of human association shifts from the political space of the city to the economic space of the house.

In 1927, in his book *Groszstadt Architektur* (The architecture of the big city), Ludwig Hilberseimer affirmed that the project for the city consists of coordination between two extremes: the overall plan for the city that would link the form of the city with its productive and economic forces, and the definition of the single inhabitable cell.[27] One of the most radical representations of this interpretation of urban management is Hilberseimer's project for the so-called Vertical City, the Hochhausstadt. Like Cerdà's plan for Barcelona, Hilberseimer's plan for the Hochhausstadt (a theoretical project that can be read as a plan for the reform of Berlin) is an attempt to establish an overall urban system rather than insisting on a composition of different city parts. In this project Hilberseimer takes a polemical stand against not only the utopian images proposed by expressionist architecture but also Le Corbusier's Contemporary City for Three Million Inhabitants (1922). In his well-known proposal, Le Corbusier seems to arrange different building types according to the figures of classical architecture: the spatiality of the typical Parisian classicist square is evoked by the space between the Cartesian skyscrapers; the layout of the Palace of Versailles is evoked by the Redents; the communitarian form of the abbey cloister is reinterpreted in the Immeubles-Villas; and, finally, the outline of Michelangelo's plan for St. Peter's is seen in the form of the train and air terminal at the city center.[28] Moreover, Le Corbusier clearly uses diverse building typologies, from the most monumental at the center to the more suburban at the periphery, and separates residential space from work space. Hilberseimer, on the other hand, uses only one building type: a hybrid of blocks and slabs in which all civic activities, such as production, living, and commerce, are superimposed rather than zoned in different locations. Thus the form of the city emerges from the repetition of a single typology, and reflects the logic of the most conventional geometry possible—that of the grid. The circulation system of the Hochhausstadt is extended uniformly in all directions by the superimposition of train lines, metro lines, trams, roads, and pedestrian streets in a tartan pattern. For Hilberseimer, typological diversification no longer seems to be an issue. Due to the extreme social mobility brought about by changing labor conditions in the modern metropolis, living standards are reduced to those of the hotel room, which is contained in an absolutely uniform slab superimposed atop a plinth comprising workshops and office space. Distributive zoning and diverse typologies disappear because the inhabitants of Hochhausstadt live, work, and move *everywhere.*

In Le Corbusier's hierarchical City for Three Million Inhabitants, programmatic diversity is attained by means of formal alternatives, but in Hilberseimer's Hochhausstadt, programmatic diversity is addressed by assembling all of the elements of the city—domestic space, office space, roads, railway lines, etc.—into one gridded system that eventually can be repeated ad infinitum. Architectural form is no longer seen as representation but as process. In the Hochhausstadt, form is devoid of any figurative or individualistic feature, guaranteeing that it will perform in the most rational, uniform way. The city is reduced to its reproductive conditions.

1.2
Ludwig Hilberseimer, Hochhausstadt, 1924.
Urbanization as a totalizing superimposition of mobility,
living, and work. Architecture is replaced by the endless
repetition of identical urban systems.

Within this frame, any distinction between public space and private space, between political space and economic space, collapses in favor of a totalizing, organic understanding of the city as devoid of any limit, where urbanity itself is conceived as one domestic space. The governing methods of economy transcend the boundaries between public space and private space, instituting the latter—the despotic administration of the house—as the principal mode of governance for the whole of urbanity. The essence of urbanization is therefore the destruction of any limit, boundary, or form that is not the infinite, compulsive repetition of its own reproduction and the consequent totalizing mechanism of control that guarantees this process of infinity.

The process of urbanization transcends not only the difference between public and private, but also any difference that matters politically, such as the difference between built space and open space, or between what Arendt identified as the three spheres of the human condition: labor, work, and "vita activa."[29] All of these differences are absorbed within a process of growth that is no longer dialectical but incremental and therefore infinite. It is not by chance that the key concepts of contemporary urbanity—such as network, landscape, globalization—share the same conceptual and ideological common ground: the infinite continuity of movement propelled by production, which systematically metabolizes anything within a process that always changes, and is thus able to preserve its stability.

From minimalism to Andy Warhol, from cybernetics to Robert Smithson, the main task of much late modern culture seems to have been the development of the idea of processing infinity through endless repetition. As the art historian Pamela Lee has suggested,[30] this can be described in terms of Hegel's concept of "bad infinity"—a sort of nightmare of the dialectical process.[31] For Hegel, "bad infinity" is the infinity that, in spite of its attempted negation of the finite—the fact that things and events have a form, a limit, and an existence—cannot avoid incarnation in the finite, which pushes toward a perennial, compulsive repetition of itself. This compulsive repetition leads to a loss of temporal specificity and historical process—that is, to the sense of *destiny* in the moment in which we happen to live. In bad infinity, everything is reduced to blind faith, to the infinite creation of new, finite things just for the sake of new things. It is creation ex nihilo, because it is patently detached from any goal other than instigating the production—through consumption—of the new.

The architectural metaproject that most radically expressed the idea of bad infinity was Archizoom's No-Stop City (1968–1972), which shows the city consumed by the infinity of urbanization.[32] This project was initially inspired by the autonomist Marxism of the 1960s, known as Operaismo.[33] As the political theorist Mario Tronti argued, it was a fatal mistake to search for the salvation of the working class independent of the development of the capitalist integration of society, because the capitalist revolution offered more advantages to the working class—the association of producers—than to the bourgeoisie itself.[34] The more society was totalized by the network of production and cooperation, the more possibilities there were for the working class to exercise a decisive political sovereignty over all of society by simply refusing society's fundamental power mechanism: the organization of work.[35] The more advanced capitalism became, the more advanced the working class's capacity to attack it would become. Consequently, Archizoom elaborated a model of extreme and total urbanization wherein technological integration was so advanced that the idea of the center as a place of financial accumulation and the periphery as a place of production would be increasingly superseded by an urban model in which production, accumulation, and consumption coincided within an ever-expanding, ever more isotropic

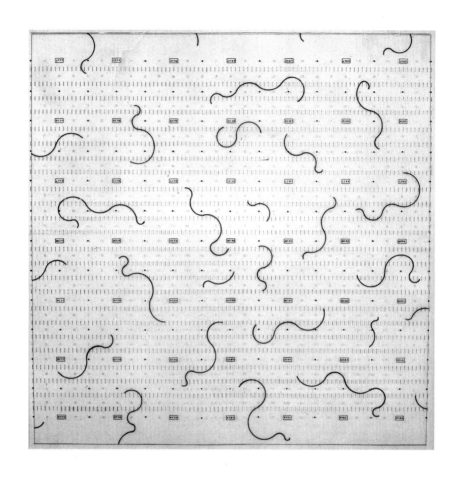

1.3
Archizoom Associati, No-Stop City, 1968–1972.
Urbanization imagined as the superimposition of three
main urban paradigms: the factory (production), the
supermarket (consumption), and the parking lot (living).

plan: urbanization. Inspired by Hilberseimer's nonfigurative urban plans, Archizoom imagined this isotropic plan as finally liberated from the various traditional figurative and spatial forms of bourgeois ideological representations of the city, and prepared for an "ultimate" clash between the workers and capitalism, implicating the entire urban infrastructure—the entire *urbs* itself.[36]

If Cerdà's *General Theory* was a progressive and reformist instrumentalization of urbanization, Archizoom's celebration of the *urbs* was intended to be "shock therapy": No-Stop City proposes a radicalization *per absurdum* of the industrial, consumer, and expansionist forces of the capitalist metropolis in the form of a continuous city with no attribute other than its infinite quantity. Extrusions of an amorphous and dispersed urban growth, the large horizontal plinths of No-Stop City show continuous carpets of urbanization within protected spaces that are artificially illuminated and air-conditioned. No-Stop City theorizes a city without difference between outside and inside, old and new, public space and private space, production space and consumption space (in No-Stop City, the parking, the factory, and the supermarket are the same mode of urban living). In this depiction of the future, everything is absorbed in the isotropic system of infrastructure: an elevator every 100 square meters, a bathroom every 50 square meters, etc. However, unlike Cerdà's criteria of infrastructure and facilities distribution, No-Stop City was not a project. Following Engels's thesis that there is no working-class city, only a working-class critique of the existing city,[37] the homogeneous plan of No-Stop City was imagined as an empirically exaggerated (and thus critical) commentary on the biopolitical mechanism of the city, where infrastructure, and thus social control, is not restricted to the factory but is everywhere. For this reason No-Stop City is neither a utopia nor a proposal for an alternative model of urbanization; rather, the hallucinatory and exaggerated descriptions of the existing conditions in which the economy reproduces its labor force are finally exposed as the ultimate core of urban culture. Thus, the salient aspect of No-Stop City—as its name declares—is its unlimited growth, its abolition of any limits, and therefore its lack of any form.

A fundamental aspect of No-Stop City is the disappearance of architecture and its replacement by furniture design, which was seen as a more effective form of urbanization because it is more flexible, and therefore more consumable and reproducible, than architecture. But if No-Stop City was imagined as the ultimate shock therapy for urbanization by its exaggeration of urbanization's consequences, in reality the tendency described by No-Stop City evolved not toward infinity and the final dissolution of the city, but rather toward a process of bad infinity. Following Hegel, the condition of the noncity proposed by No-Stop City perpetually undergoes a process of compulsive repetition, in which any complexity or contradiction, any difference or novelty, is an incentive for the infinite reproduction of the system itself and thus for its stasis. For this reason, in spite of its aspiration to represent per absurdum the capitalist process of urbanization, and in spite of its theoretical purity and radicalism, No-Stop City ultimately "succeeded" in prophesying a world in which human associations are ruled only by the logic of economy and rendered in terms of diagrams and growth statistics. Like No-Stop City, the actual modern city has become a shopping mall, where value-free pluralism and diversity—the totalizing features of its space—have made urbanization the perfect space of mass voluntary servitude to the apolitical democracy imposed by the market. While beginning as a politically radical project, No-Stop City has come to prefigure how bad infinity has ensnared humanity within the logic of indefinite growth as a means of development, constantly aspiring to the new and different, and thereby forcing humanity to identically repeat its own condition.

Cerdà's *General Theory*, Hilberseimer's *Groszstadt Architektur*, and Archizoom's No-Stop City theorized urbanization as the ultimate and inevitable fate of the contemporary city. They imagined this fate with the best intentions: for them, liberation from the city meant liberation from its traditional powers and hierarchies and the full realization of what even for Marx was the ultimate mastery of society: economy. Their proposed models and descriptions imagined an isotropic geography of infrastructure that would homogenize the entire urban territory.

According to Cerdà, Hilberseimer, and Archizoom, there was no need for monuments, forms, or exceptions to the rule. That rule was both the ever-expanding web of the network and the individual capsule of the house: that which maintains the reproduction of work. However, even if Cerdà's *General Theory*, Hilberseimer's *Groszstadt Architektur*, and No-Stop City are correctly understood as defining the aspirations and, in some respect, the reality of the contemporary urban condition, they could not predict two fundamental "collateral effects" of urbanization, which at first sight seem to contradict the logic of bad infinity: the *enclave* and the *landmark*. These "collateral effects" seem to be the basic elements of another metaproject of contemporary urbanization, in which captivity and iconographic diversity play a fundamental role: Rem Koolhaas's City of the Captive Globe.[38] Conceived in 1972, the City of the Captive Globe is a representation of Manhattan and its culture of congestion, and also, as Koolhaas himself declared, the de facto ideological and conceptual blueprint of *Delirious New York*, which he published six years later.[39]

The City of the Captive Globe describes an urban condition that, through the simultaneous explosion of human density and invasion of new technologies—precisely what constitutes the core

1.4
Rem Koolhaas, The City of the Captive Globe, 1972.
Urbanization imagined as a collection of different,
and competing, built "ideologies." The more
different the ideologies, the more the urban order
that maintains them is reinforced. Here the potential
agonism between built forms is absorbed by the
managerial order of the urban layout.

of urbanization—perpetually challenges its limits as a city. In the project the Manhattan grid is represented by a potentially infinite series of plots, each composed of a base of heavy polished stone. Koolhaas calls these bases "ideological laboratories" in which different kinds of metropolitan consciousness are formed.[40] Each base is a state of exception (as defined in chapter 4) and, as Koolhaas writes, each is equipped to "suspend unwelcome laws, undeniable truths, and to create extreme artificial conditions."[41] The suspension of any general law or truth is manifested in the deliberately and radically different architectures that sit on top of each base. These architectures constitute a Valhalla of Koolhaas's favorite archetypal buildings, such as the RCA Building, Superstudio's Isograms, El Lissitzky's Lenin Tribune, Malevich's Tektonics, Mies's typical American building complex, and even an elevator. In Koolhaas's city these archetypes, once singular avant-garde gestures or forerunners of ideal cities and worlds, are now "lobotomized" from their original context (whether real or ideological) and placed on top of a block that mediates between them and the horizontal grid that makes possible their coexistence within the same urban space. The aim of the City of the Captive Globe is to resolve the inevitable schism between the permanency of the urban system—the combination of horizontal and vertical circulation provided by the grid and the elevator— and the radical pluralism required by the metropolis represented by the eclectic skyline, where avant-garde archetypes of the city are "accepted" and reduced to "icons." The City of the Captive Globe allows what Koolhaas later, in describing China's Pearl River Delta region, would call the "city of exacerbated differ- ences"[42]—to the point that the state of exception contained by each plot becomes the norm of the city itself. The more change and exception are allowed, the more the urban principle is rein- forced, because the axioms of Koolhaas's city consist of the grid, which equalizes differences within an isotropic network; the lobotomy, which largely eliminates the relationship between the "inside" (architecture) and the "outside" (urbanization); and the schism, which reduces every plot to a self-sufficient enclave that, by retaining its function, can host any ideology without affecting the general principle of urbanization.

Like Cerdà's idea of urbanization, Hilberseimer's principle of the plan, and Archizoom's No-Stop City, the City of the Captive Globe is based on an isotropic principle and the potential for infinite development, but unlike these models it has a center, which is the square of the Captive Globe itself. If the project is a portrait of Manhattan, then the square of the Captive Globe—which for Koolhaas reinforces the identity of the city as a miniature of the world itself—is analogous to Central Park's role in New York. This void—a carpet of synthetic nature—nullifies the most evident attribute of the metropolis—its density—to dialectically reinforce its opposite: urban congestion. Koolhaas called his model an "archipelago": the grid is a sea and the plots are islands. The more different the values celebrated by each island, the more united and total the grid or sea that surrounds them. Hence, the plots are not simply buildings but are cities in miniature or, as Koolhaas calls them, quoting Oswald Mathias Ungers, "cities within cities."

Indeed, the project for the City of the Captive Globe, and, one can argue, the whole structure of *Delirious New York*, are heavily influenced by the urban ideas of Ungers, with whom Koolhaas collaborated between 1972 and 1975, first while studying at Cornell and then at the Institute for Architecture and Urban Studies, where he wrote his book. Though the book is a retroactive manifesto for Manhattan, the city is not described in its entirety but rather is represented through a series of exceptional and idiosyncratic architectural visions, such as Coney Island, the RCA Building, and Rockefeller Center, and through the contrasting ideologies of Dalí and Le Corbusier. Similarly, in the 1960s and 1970s Ungers worked on several projects (both with his office and with his students at TU Berlin and Cornell) based on the idea of the city of contrasting parts. In each project he developed architecture as an urban composition in miniature that would contain the complexity of the city as a whole. The city, and its architecture, would be not a unitary system but what Ungers (quoting the fifteenth-century German theologian and philosopher Nicholas of Cusa) called a "coincidentia oppositorum"—that is, the coincidence, or composition, of not just different parts but opposing ones, which leads to a critical unity.[43] Ungers's concept of the archipelago as a city made of radically different parts juxtaposed in the same space was the primary influence on Koolhaas's idea of New York as an urban paradigm. While for Ungers the parts that compose the city are meant to oppose each other, and are thus bound to the dialectical principle that something is united by being separated, for Koolhaas, the difference between the blocks is difference itself, where variations can unfold infinitely without affecting the general principle. In Koolhaas's Manhattan archipelago, difference is reinforced by the total schism between the image of architecture—where anything goes—and the functioning of the island, which ultimately is dictated by the grid and the elevator, and which indeed "lobotomizes" the forms of the buildings. Yet the space of the building in Koolhaas's City of the Captive Globe is not really that of an island, where the relationship between inside (terra firma) and outside (the sea) is vital and open to different approaches, but is more like an enclave, where the enclave's strict dependence on the regime of accessibility and circulation is compensated for by the overdose of ideology and iconography provided by the landmark.

The enclave is a restricted space that makes the urban territory uneven. Unlike the Greek *polis*, which was a kind of enclave because its inside was clearly separated and self-sufficient from the outside, the space of the contemporary enclave as exemplified by Koolhaas's Manhattan landmarks is not truly separated from the outside but is simply segregated; in other words, while access to its space is restricted, its existence depends on the functioning of the network of urbanization. The enclave can be understood as a direct consequence of the economic mastery of capitalist accumulation, because capitalism always connects and integrates the urban territory when it must absorb, exploit, control, and organize labor and transform it into profit; but it also always segregates when it comes time to accumulate and distribute that profit. The social discrimination dictated by the selective space of the enclave is, in the end, based not on politics but on the total sovereignty of economy in the form of urban management, which in turn can use other criteria, such as politics, to reinforce the effectiveness of organization and discrimination. A similar phenomenon can be applied to the contemporary use of the landmark, which in the City of the Captive Globe is represented by the exuberant iconic spectacle of the city skyline and its divorce from the logic of the whole. Contrary to the idea of a "nonfigurative" city as imagined by Archizoom, the City of the Captive Globe can be interpreted as a prediction of contemporary urbanization in which pluralism and diversity are celebrated (and exaggerated) within the strict spatial logic of the enclave. Bound to the regime of the economy, this logic of inclusion/exclusion dissolves the potential dialectical conflict among the parts of the city, and transforms confrontation and its solution—coexistence—into the indifference of cohabitation, which indeed is the way of living in urbanization. If, as stated before, the city began as a dilemma between *civitas* and *urbs*, between the possibility of encounter (the possibility of conflict) and the possibility of security, it has ended up as completely absorbed by the infinite process of urbanization and its despotic nature.

Facing this scenario of infinite urbanization—which today is no longer just theory but daily practice—I would argue that the time has come to drastically counter the very idea of urbanization. For this reason I propose a partisan view of the city against the totalizing space of urbanization. In order to formulate a meta-critique of urbanization as the incarnation of infinity and the current stasis of economic power over the city, I propose to reassess the concepts of the political and the formal as they unfold into an idea of architecture that critically responds to the idea of urbanization. In this proposal, the political is equated with the formal, and the formal is finally rendered as the idea of a *limit*.

Arendt writes, "Politics is based on the fact of human plurality."[44] Unlike desires, imagination, or metaphysics, politics does not exist as a human essence but only happens outside of man. "Man is apolitical. Politics arises between men, and so quite outside man," she writes. "There is no real political substance. Politics arises in what lies between men and it is established as a relationship."[45] The political occurs in the decision of how to articulate the relationship, the *infra* space, the space in between. The space in between is a constituent aspect of the concept of form, found in the contraposition of parts. As there is no way to think the political within man himself, there is also no way to think the space in between in itself. The space in between can only materialize as a space of confrontation between parts. Its existence can only be decided by the parts that form its edges.

In the dual terms of Carl Schmitt, the space in between is formed by the decision of who is a friend and who is an enemy.[46] This decision does not exist "as found" in between the parts, but arises from the position taken by the parts that form this space. The word *decision* derives from the Latin *caedere*: to cut, to cut the links. To decide one's own counterpart means to consciously struggle for autonomy, but in a way in which, through this gesture of cutting, one also realizes an inner belonging to what one is detaching from. In this sense, the notion of agonism—the counterpositioning of parts—functions as a critical mirroring of oneself via the other, to the extent that it is possible to say that to make a collective claim of political autonomy one must first declare one's counterpart. In other words, there is no way to claim autonomy without first asking what we are affirming ourselves against as political subjects—as parts.[47] After the period of great ideological conflicts such as the cold war between capitalism and socialism, this dialectical process of political recognition has been absorbed by, and has vanished within, the political correctness of pluralism and difference, to the extent that the figure of the enemy has been transformed into an evil figure par excellence—what Schmitt calls the "total enemy."[48] In contemporary common opinion, the word *enemy* evokes a bloody and noncivic way of being. From an economic point of view, agonism as such is useless and damaging, so it must be made into competition, or even war, to make it profitable. In turn, the parts of society that, facing the existing order of civil society, find themselves in a position of agonism, no longer understand their struggle as an implicit recognition of a counterpart, but see it as antagonism, as an endless struggle without any acknowledgment of the adversary. Given this mentality, we have to remember that the figure of the enemy—understood not as *inimicus* but as *hostis*[49]—is one of the greatest existential figures of human civilization. The notion of agonism renders, in an essential way, the idea of oneself not as a value-free atom of society but as an active part capable of distinction, judgment, and action toward something declared as its opposite. The figure of the enemy is the form *per via negativa* through which we recognize ourselves. There cannot be civilization without recognition of the enemy, without the possibility of division, difference, decision within the universal space of cohabitation—the possibility of deciding one's destiny. Schmitt affirmed that the recognition of one's opposite is instrumental to avoiding self-deception. For this reason, in Schmitt's definition of the political, the figure of the friend is conspicuously over-looked, or to be more accurate, remains in the background, because Schmitt mostly focuses on the enemy. As Heinrich Meyer suggests, this is because, according to Schmitt's definition, the friend, by virtue of his benevolence, cannot help but confirm our situation of self-deception.[50] The enemy, on the other hand, estranges us from our familiar self-perception and gives us back the sharp contour of our own figure, of our own *position*. What counters us inevitably constitutes the knowledge of our own limit, our own form. To answer the pressing question of who is an adversary and who is not is inevitably to be political—that is, to judge. As Arendt writes, "Political thought is essentially based on judgment."[51] The sphere of the political is the sphere in which a part, a group of individuals, acquires knowledge of itself in the form of knowing what it is, what it ought to be, what it wants, and what it does not want. The political is an attitude (to act in relationship to something); it consists of knowledge (knowing who, and what, to counterpose), and indicates a task (to transform conflict into coexistence without exaggerating, or denying, the reasons for the conflict itself). The political cannot be reduced to conflict per se; it indicates the possibility of conflict and as such calls for its solution. Even if it means slightly confounding the terms of Hegel's dialectic, the political realizes the solution of conflict not by a synthesis of the confronting parts, but by rec-ognizing the opposition as a *composition* of parts. This suggests that it is possible to theorize a phenomenological and symbolic coincidence between political action and the making of the form of an object. Both deal with the fundamental question of defining the limits that constitute related, but different, parts. It is from this vantage point—the question of a composition of parts, the question of limits posed through knowledge of the other—that I propose to redefine the concept of the formal.

The Latin *forma* stands for two Greek words with quite different meanings: *eidos*, or abstract form, and *morphè*, or visible form. In its very origin the word *form* seems to contain the dispute between those who give priority to the visibility of things as a fundamental datum of experience and those who give priority to the inner structure of experience itself as the factor that determines how visible things are. Since this dispute runs the risk of being reduced to the abused dichotomy of form/content—form as visible container with invisible content—I propose a definition of form that transcends the duality of abstract/visible. Thus, analogous with Schmitt's argument in *The Concept of the Political*, I do not discuss form as such, but rather its application as criteria, as a concept: the *formal*.

The formal can be defined as the experience of limit, as the relationship between the "inside" and the "outside." By the inside, I mean the position assumed by an acting subject; by the outside, I mean the *datum*, the situation, the state of things in which the subject acts. Action versus situation or subject versus datum: these are the poles through which the notion of the formal materializes.[52] Therefore, form is the implicit limit that inevitably exists between action and datum—*of action's grasp of the world*, to paraphrase the Swiss philosopher Jeanne Hersch, who wrote one of the most penetrating books on the idea of form.[53] Hersch maintains that the notion of form is a paradox, or rather, that it "simultaneously indicates unity on the one hand and, on the other, spatial differentiation, a partial character, limitation, determination, and change."[54] The inherent tension in the concept of form lies entirely in the subjective will of a unity, or rather the subjective will of knowing through a conceptual a priori, through form's own limits, and the differentiation that this a priori necessarily entails in the indefinite space of the possible. In this sense, form is above all a cognitive instrument. Not despite but through this paradox—as Hersch maintains—form exists from the moment it represents the tension from an inside toward an outside. We can argue that the formal indicates a decision on how the "inside" relates itself to the "outside," and how the latter is delineated from within. The formal essentially involves an act of spatial determination, of (de)limitation. Within this understanding of the formal it is possible to make the following propositions.[55]

Inasmuch as the formal is defined in terms of limits rather than self-sufficiency, it is fundamentally relational. In its finitude and specificity, it implies the existence of something outside of itself. In being concerned with "itself," it necessarily concerns the "other." For this reason, the formal is against totality and generic conceptions of multiplicity. The formal is thus a veritable representation of the political, since the political is the agonistic space of real confrontation, of the others. As such, the formal is a partisan idea. From this perspective we can say that it is precisely the condition of the *absoluteness* of the form of an object (*absolute* being understood in its original meaning, "separated") that implies what exists outside of it. Like the concept of the political, the concept of the formal expresses the condition of a *cum-positio* of parts.

In this condition of a composition of parts, the concept of the formal and the concept of the political coincide and can be posited against notions such as urban space, urban landscape, and network, which are facts but also the very ideological manifestation of the idea of urbanization. These notions imply the integration and dissolution of difference, while the concept of the political and the concept of the formal indicate the possibility of the composition of difference by assuming the limits of parts as their constituency. Consequently, both the political and the formal contain the idea of the whole *per via negativa*, by virtue of being absolute parts.

To what idea of the city do concepts such as the formal and the political refer? What is the form of the city that incarnates the political composition of parts? Before addressing these questions, I would like to emphasize that these criteria are reformulated here against the tide of contemporary descriptions of the city, where "realism" and "postcriticality" have become excuses for denying responsibility and surrendering to the economic forces of urbanization. The coincidence between the formal and the political as defined here is not meant literally to formalize a city against the fluidity of urbanization, but rather to sharpen the ways in which we critically approach the political in order to define a possibility for the formal. This possibility can only occur if we search for a form of reference that can critically reconstruct an idea of the whole—the integrity of the city as a political manifestation that is *critical of* urbanization itself, while also *within* urbanization. One thing must be clear: there is no way back from urbanization, and the search for the contemporary agora is a pathetic endeavor that only manifests the weakness of our political understanding of the city. At the same time, we must build the political and formal integrity of the city, which consists not of a nostalgic reconstruction of an ideal place which has never existed,[56] but of a clear set of criteria and forms of reference. What could be a form of reference for a renewed political and formal understanding of the city and its architecture?

If we do not appeal to peremptory images such as those urbanization provides of globalization, the governance of the market, and so on, it becomes quite difficult to synthesize the aspirations and ideas that constitute the evolution of what we still call the contemporary city into a simple form of reference. Without general projects such as those we have seen before, every recent attempt to build a representative and intelligible image of the urban phenomena has been preempted by the complex, cognitive, hybrid, and often intentionally vague metabolism that is implied in the more recent descriptions of the city—descriptions continuously subjugated to the appearance of new concerns, and thus more and more averse to building interpretative models that are capable of placing themselves beyond the rhetoric of *change*. This cognitive metabolism, exemplified by terms such as *mutation*, *transurbanism*, *postmetropolis*, *city in transition*, *city on the move*[57]—terms that have characterized fundamental moments in reflections on the city in recent years—gives place to a certain imaginary in which it is impossible to identify the parts that constitute the ensemble of the city. In the absence of a representable whole, the individuality or singularity of parts is dissolved into a vision dominated by the figure of the fragment, which renders any representation of the world impossible unless it is through the paradoxical use of comprehensive and totalizing concepts such as *globalization*, *dispersion*, *congestion*, or *density*. Because these concepts are unable to comprehend the multiplicity, they celebrate it, hence allowing for a representation in which the forms of the manifold themselves paradoxically disappear.

Given this situation, I am not concerned with the further mappings of urbanization and their complexities and contradictions. Rather, I am concerned with the possibility of constituting other criteria for an interpretation of the idea of the city and its architecture based on the concepts of the political and the formal.

Instead of resorting to cognitive frameworks such as vision, scenario, and utopia, which often reduce the world to simplistic and totalizing representations, I am proposing a way in which any general construction of the idea of the city is conceived by starting from the limits of architectural form itself. I am therefore opening, in a different way, the problem of form as the critical relationship between architecture and the city by revisiting a "city project" that is not considered as such: the persistence of the form of the plinth in all of Mies van der Rohe's major projects.

To oppose Mies's architecture, which is bound to the scale of the building, to projects or visions that focus on overall urban systems may seem incongruous. Unlike the previous examples, but also unlike many architects of his time, from Le Corbusier to Frank Lloyd Wright, Mies never proposed a general plan, a general model, or a general project of reform for the city or even a utopian scheme for the city. It is even more problematic to talk about Mies within a discourse on the political and the formal, for Mies seems to be the most remote reference for such argument. He rarely expressed positions, or even opinions, on politics, and he always showed a caustic attitude toward theoretical discourses on form in architecture, to the point that historian Werner Oechslin defined Mies as the greatest antiformalist architect of the twentieth century.[58]

Mies focused on architecture as a "distanced" accomplishment of its purpose: the framing of space. Yet, as Manfredo Tafuri has pointed out, the silent forms through which Mies pursued this goal are far from idealistic.[59] Especially in his American corporate projects, Mies allowed the attributes of industrial technology—the famous I-beams used in the Seagram Building facade, for example—to enter and envelop his architecture. In this way the forces of urbanization in the form of the mass production of building technology became the very appearance of his architecture.

In this regard it is important to mention Mies's lifetime friendship and collaboration with Hilberseimer. Hilberseimer's idea of the city consisted of the most extreme reduction of city form to the logic of urban management. Although he opted, shortly after his Hochhausstadt proposal and later in his American period, for a more dispersed model of urbanization, Hilberseimer radicalized the generic forms of settlements to the point that, as Albert Pope has pointed out, his urban plans were made not for "form" but of "space."[60] This is evident in the way Hilberseimer drew his urban plans. Only the systems of circulation and the natural features of the territory are figured in these plans; all the rest—the city, its places, its borders, its forms—are completely dissolved into the "urban system." The diagrammatic minimalism through which Hilberseimer represented his plans is much more than a simple technique of drawing. Such graphic minimalism amounts to a highly evocative rendering of the very ethos of urbanization—its composition of systems and flows rather than places and forms. Hilberseimer's drawings suggest a complete acceptance of the main value of urbanization—that of management—yet they express this without any formal commentary.

Mies's architectural language is not at odds with Hilberseimer's "regional patterns" of urbanization.[61] The "silence" of Mies's architecture seems to evolve directly from the "generic city" evoked by Hilberseimer. The same gray unaesthetic logic that guides Hilberseimer in confronting the complex and ineffable forces of urbanization is implied in Mies's approach to these architectural complexes. For this reason Hilberseimer's "generic city" can be seen as the backdrop to Mies's projects, which seem to be the most appropriate form within Hilberseimer's ruthless reduction of the city to the logic of urbanization.

Neither an architecture of hope nor of celebration, Mies's buildings remain stubborn yet docile and simple orthogonal forms within the generic space of the modern metropolis. Their apparent indifference to context is paradoxically their true contextual quality, which reflects, in the most literal and objective terms, precisely what one cannot see: the generic space of exchange and reproduction behind the appearance of figural diversity.[62] The "silence" of Mies's architecture has often been interpreted by historians and critics as reflecting and incorporating the uprooting nature of modernity while defining a critical distance from it.[63] These interpretations range from the aesthetic of renunciation proposed by Tafuri, who saw in Mies's American projects the explicit interiorization of the abstraction of social life itself in the form of a paradoxical formal autonomy *per via negativa*, to Massimo Cacciari's reading of Mies's abstraction (and of modern architecture) as a conscious image of fulfilled nihilism; to Michael Hays's use of Mies as an example of critical architecture, posited as both a radical detachment from all that is outside architecture and a reflection of the conditions that permit such distance; to Detlef Mertins's rendering of Mies's redeeming use of technology; to Sven-Olov Wallenstein's interpretation of Mies's silence not as an act of negativity and rejection, but an act of harboring a plethora of words to come: "the promise or rather the threat of a new and pliant discourse that in many aspects forms the very element of the world today."[64]Yet, with the notable exceptions of the German critic Fritz Neumeyer[65]and Oswald Mathias Ungers,[66] these canonical readings seem mostly to have focused on the Miesian motif of the building envelope, while giving less importance to the element that defined all of Mies's projects: the careful placement of buildings through the use of the plinth. From his early suburban houses in Germany to his corporate office complexes in the United States, the simple, bounded form of the plinth (which can be interpreted as an abstract version of the Greek stylobate) is the precondition for nearly all of Mies's designs. If, as Neumeyer argues, the pavilion-like quality of Mies's buildings seems to follow Karl Friedrich Schinkel's attempt to elevate the freestanding architectural object as an analogous form encompassing bourgeois space (as opposed to the imperial claims of baroque architecture), then the plinth gives this appropriation a self-defined limit. This is evident in projects such as the Riehl House (1907), the Barcelona Pavilion (1929), the Seagram Building (1954–1958), and the New National Gallery in Berlin (1962–1968). By putting emphasis on the building site, the plinth inevitably makes the site a limit for what it contains. The isotropic order of industrialization evoked by the building envelopes is contrasted by their siting, framed by the plinth. Moreover, the way the plinth reorganizes the connection between a building and its site affects not only one's experience of what is placed *on* the plinth, but also—and especially—one's experience of the city that is *outside* the plinth. One of the most remarkable things felt by anyone climbing a Mies plinth, whether in New York or in Berlin, is the experience of turning one's back to the building in order to look at the city. Suddenly, and for a brief moment, one is estranged from the flows and organizational patterns that animate the city, yet still confronting them. In this way Mies's plinths reinvent urban space as an archipelago of limited urban artifacts. It is this emphasis on finiteness and separateness that makes artifacts like these the most intense manifestation of the political in the city. There is no doubt that Mies's projects, especially those executed for corporations, are the embodiment of the values that have produced the logic of urbanization. And yet, precisely because Mies's architecture has this source, its emphasis on separateness and self-limitation seems even more intensely political.

While the materiality and composition of Mies's envelopes reproduce the attributes of the generic city, their placement on a

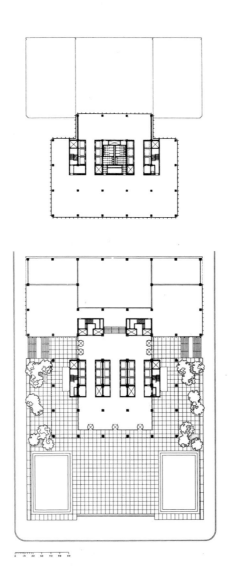

1.5
Ludwig Mies van der Rohe, Seagram Building, 1954–1958.
The generic attributes of architecture framed by the plinth.
The gesture of the plinth implies a city made by self-limited,
and thus countering, forms rather than by ubiquitous flows.

plinth presents these attributes not as ubiquitous, but as sensual and finite objects. And while Mies's buildings assume the generic attributes of production, his insistence on framing and limiting proposes these attributes not as norms, but as architectural *states of exception* that force the generic to conform to the finite form of location. In this way the forces of urbanization are made explicit and are made to define their own position as agonistic form.

In Mies's architecture the idea of location and the sense of "place" that this embodies are not the outcome of some sort of genius loci or other form of place "authenticity." The singularity of location, and thus of place, that the plinth evokes is the direct outcome of the same generic architecture of its context. Mies's urban spaces make no attempt to decorate their architecture with attributes that visually mimic the city within their microcosm. Mies's urban spaces are literally made by those materials and forms that one would expect at the entrance to a modern building: the gridlike tiling of the pavement, the freestanding elevator shafts, pools of water, or green grass, some benches. Yet it is the composition and framing of these elements within the plinth that estrange them from the ordinary, and render them as unique experiences without any aura of formal uniqueness.

In the age of "biopolitics" and "geopolitics," where political subjectivity is constantly reformulated in ever more complex and impalpable terms, one can ask whether the bodily experience of form and location can make sense at all. But this is precisely the point. Today a possible and radical counteraction to the ubiquity of the management of space in all its forms can be proposed only by reaffirming in the most radical terms the most graspable junctures through which space must be made. A noniconic gesture such as the plinth seems to open an analogical crack in urban space even when it has been totalized by the managerial forces of urbanization. The plinth introduces a stoppage into the smoothness of urban space, thus evoking the possibility of understanding urban space not as ubiquitous, pervasive, and tyrannical, but as something that can be framed, limited, and thus potentially situated as a thing among other things. While buildings assume the ineffable attributes of urbanization, the plinth limits these attributes to a finite location. Moreover, unlike the wall, a form like the plinth is a frame that does not simply separate or isolate; it also recuperates in subtle ways the difference that the modern city has subsumed within its generic space: the symbolic possibility of confrontation.

Unlike Cerdà, Hilberseimer, Archizoom, and Koolhaas, Mies is concerned not only with the generic quality of this form but also with its limit, with the finitude of its location. Architecture is thus reinvented by absorbing the *compulsion to repeat*, which is the essential trait of capitalist civilization, while increasing architecture's function as a frame, as a limit both to itself and to the forces and interests it represents. Mies not only developed a particular model of architecture, he also introduced a particular attitude toward the city.

Today, against the ubiquity of design and its embedded organizational complex, this attitude toward framing and limiting needs to be developed both as a literal material form of architecture and as a political principle of design. Rather than open-ended growth, *limiting*, or the confrontation among parts, should be conceived as the fundamental metaproject that gives form to architecture's critical position toward the city. There is no question that the idea of limits implies issues that go far beyond the scope of architecture and its project, and involves the complex ecology of political and economic space. Yet, like the archetypes we have seen before, the task of architecture is to *reify*—that is, to transform into public, generic, and thus graspable *common* things—the political organization of space, of which architectural form is not just the consequence but also one of the most powerful and influential political examples. In this way, absolute architecture as a finite form is not simply the tautological claim of its literal object; it is also the example for a city no longer driven by the ethos of expansion and inclusion but by the positive idea of limits and confrontation.

By clearly exposing their limits, architectural parts confront each other and form an agonistic plurality, becoming a site where judgment through difference is again possible. Here the formal clearly becomes the political essence of the city. Architecture no longer follows urbanization's despotic routine; rather, it is a precondition for urbanization, a project that reconstructs through itself the formal and the political sense of the city.

In this sense, Mies's interventions, especially the formal principle enumerated by projects such as the Seagram Building in New York, the Federal Center in Chicago, Westmount Square in Montreal, and the Toronto-Dominion Centre, are here assumed as examples for a city conceived as a group of islands within a sea of urbanization.

These interventions can be reduced to a prototype—a set of finite volumes arranged within a clearly demarcated space, the plinth. I believe that these interventions constitute one of the highest examples of an absolute architecture, for they make clear its separateness, provoking the agonistic experience of the city. The city made by agonistic parts is the archipelago.

An archipelago is a group of islands set in a sea that simultaneously unites and divides them. Yet the archipelago is not just a collection of different parts that share proximity; the form of the archipelago presupposes that its parts, even in their *absolute separation*, are moved by an *absent* center, toward which each island, in communion with the others, is oriented without claiming possession of this center.[67] The absent center is the locus of

1.6
Ludwig Mies van der Rohe, Toronto-Dominion Centre,
Toronto, 1963–1969. The possibility of an absolute
architecture as the separation and self-containment
of generic forms.

confrontation among the islands. Confrontation is both what attracts the islands toward each other and what separates them, preventing their coalescence into a single mass. Analogously, the absent center of the archipelago is the political form of the city, which is continually redefined by the limits, separation, and confrontation of its parts, just as the relationship between the islands and the sea is an important aspect of the archipelago. In this framework, Mies's interventions should be seen as the method of making these parts, not their style. As I have said, the sea is the extensive space of urbanization, its all-embracing connectiveness, the space of management of anything that constitutes our civilization. There is no other way to exceed this sea if not from within, by absorbing and forcing its attributes into finite, clearly separated parts

Like the forms of Mies's complexes, the architecture of the parts of the archipelago must be made of the attributes of urbanization—the common ethos of our civilization. By being forced into a form, these aspects will inevitably define a position within the endless space of urbanization. Through the emerging position of a part, the political and the formal in architecture can be reconstructed.

What sort of architecture incarnates the archipelago? The iconic building—which affirms its own singular presence through the appearance of its image, and today constitutes one of the primary expressions of architectural culture at the scale of the city—cannot be a valid part of the city. Even in putting aside problems of morality, issues of taste, and the gratuitous character of its forms, the iconic building cannot be considered an exemplary *part* of the city because its *economic* principle is to be unique and unrepeatable. Since it is no longer the state but the corporation that builds these *grands projets*, the iconic building responds to a demand for uniqueness as an emblem of market competitiveness. The huge variety of these buildings subscribes to one main criterion: to obey the despotic law of difference and novelty—precisely the attributes that fuel the bad infinity of labor for the sake of production and profit. In the economy of the iconic building, what is considered "productive" is the personality of the architect, his or her creative ego, which is exploited and used by the corporation to oppose the difficult whole of the polis—the space in which difference is not infinite variation or commercial competition, but rather a confrontation of parts. The confrontation of parts can be achieved only based on common and existing aspects of the city, not ex nihilo creation of the new. Through the exemplary and exceptional clarity of the compositional gesture, a true part of the city recognizes and represents its typical aspects. The part is *absolute*; it stands in solitude, yet it takes a position with regard to the whole from which it has been separated. The architecture of the archipelago must be an absolute architecture, an architecture that is defined by and makes clear the presence of *limits* which define the city. An absolute architecture is one that recognizes whether these limits are a product (and a camouflage) of economic exploitation (such as the enclaves determined by uneven economic redistribution) or whether they are the pattern of an ideological will to separation within the *common* space of the city. Instead of dreaming of a perfectly integrated society that can only be achieved as the supreme realization of urbanization and its avatar, capitalism, an absolute architecture must recognize the political separateness that can potentially, within the sea of urbanization, be manifest through the borders that define the possibility of the city. An absolute architecture must map these borders, understand them, formalize them, and thus reinforce them so that they can be clearly confronted and judged. Instead of being an icon of diversity per se, an absolute architecture must refuse any impetus to novelty and accept the possibility of being an instrument of separation, and thus of political action.

If one were to summarize life in a city and life in a building in one gesture, it would have to be that of passing through borders. Every moment of our existence is a continuous movement through space defined by walls. Architects cannot define urbanization: how program evolves, how movement performs, how flows unfold, how change occurs. The only program that can reliably be attributed to architecture is its specific inertia in the face of urbanization's mutability, its status as the manifestation of a clearly singular place. If the ubiquitous nature of mobility and integration is the essence of urbanization, the singularity of places is the essence of a city. We cannot return to a preurban world, but within the present urban situation there is the possibility to redefine the meaning of the city as a site of confrontation and thus of coexistence. In this sense architecture is a constructive and theoretical apparatus whose "publicness" consists in its possibility of separating, and thus forming the space of coexistence within the city. For this reason, architecture has no option but to express itself through a language that is radically and consciously appropriate, that is clear in its goals and its cause, and is able to represent and institutionalize the business of living as a value that is at once universal and singular. Architecture can have no other goal than that of relentless inquiry into the singularity of finite parts—the very singularity by which it constitutes the city. Architecture must address the city even when the city has no goal for architecture. For the city is ultimately the only object for and method of architectural investigation: decisions about the form of the city are the only way to answer the question, Why architecture?

2 THE GEOPOLITICS OF THE IDEAL VILLA
ANDREA PALLADIO AND THE PROJECT OF AN ANTI-IDEAL CITY

In 1944 Rudolf Wittkower published two essays on Andrea Palladio's architecture. The essays, later included in his book *Architectural Principles in the Age of Humanism*, featured eleven schematic drawings of Palladio's villas that Wittkower used to reinforce his argument for reading Renaissance architecture in terms of irreducible rules or principles.[1] These drawings showed that architectural artifacts such as Palladio's villas were not merely episodic formal studies but were systematic variations of the same compositional logic. Architectural principles were thus implicitly proposed as an intellectual framework for architectural form, superior to the functional, programmatic, or aesthetic goals to which architectural history was then still bound.

As a core component of architecture's emerging historiography, Wittkower's reading of Renaissance architecture quickly proved to be influential far beyond academic historical scholarship. Within postwar reconstruction in England, for example, his project established a point of reference for a generation of architects searching for formal legitimacy beyond the technocratic impetus of functionalist modernism. In particular, his drawings, reducing Palladian villas to proportional and spatial schemes, offered the possibility of defining a more profound rationality than could be provided simply by technology. This commitment to seeing and interpreting a contemporary condition through a

Renaissance precedent was reinforced five years later (and more radically still) by Colin Rowe, whose "Mathematics of the Ideal Villa" famously established a comparison between Palladio's Villa Foscari in Malcontenta and Le Corbusier's Villa Stein in Garches.[2] While Wittkower's impact on a wider, contemporary architectural discourse was as unsuspected as it was unintentional, Rowe's iconoclastic comparison of two villas—one from the sixteenth century, the other from the twentieth—seems to have been a deliberate attempt to interfere with the trajectory of postwar architectural modernism. This desire to subvert is seen not only in his argument for the comparable nature of Renaissance and modern architecture, but also in his pointing to the possibility of a rigorous close reading of architectural form independent of its historical circumstances. For this reason, Rowe deliberately extrapolates the villas of Palladio and Le Corbusier from their geographical and political context; he even argues that the architects' lyrical site descriptions celebrating their best-known villas—"La Rotonda" and the Villa Savoye at Poissy—offer too easy a point of entry for comparison. In this way, Rowe's text reinforces Wittkower's radical denial of Palladio's site specificity, apparent in the removal of the *barchesse* (barns) in his schematic drawings of the villas. These adjoining loggias were adapted from local Venetian agricultural sheds and were an essential component of Palladio's villas, providing both a sense of context and a semiotic distinction that allowed these buildings to be classified as villas rather than palaces. The *barchesse*, in this sense, are Palladio's geopolitical context because they figure as the key metonymical register for the whole typology.

Palladio's villas themselves were commissioned at the high point of widespread social and economic reforms advanced by the Serenissima Republic in the sixteenth century, and their particular formal composition—a central palace flanked by two barns—is deeply embedded in the political, social, and formal impetus of these reforms. If, as James S. Ackerman has argued, the villa is one the most radically ideological architectures because it hides its economic dependency on the city by claiming self-sufficiency within the countryside, then Palladio's palace-plus-*barchesse* composition openly signals the villa's relation with its regional and agricultural economic context.[3] This immediately suggests an alternative interpretation of Palladio's architecture to the ones advanced by Wittkower and Rowe. This counter position does not define Palladio's relevance to contemporary discourse in terms of proportion or the "mathematics" of its architectural composition, but reads the villa as one element within a larger, latent project. Rather than taking Palladio's "ideal" as a model for an equally ideal urban configuration, it views the geography and politics of the villa as a framework for rethinking and retheorizing the significance of Palladio's work as a project for an anti-ideal city.

First, however, let's deal with the name, Palladio—bombastic and slightly ridiculous in its overloaded pretension. This was the name conferred on Andrea della Gondola when he was already in his thirties, having completed a long apprenticeship in a stonemason's workshop. The man who named him—the Renaissance poet, humanist, and diplomat Giangiorgio Trissino—was making clear from the outset that Palladio was invested with a program.[4] For Trissino, this program was the reinvention of Vicenza as a model for an imperial Roman city—that is, in his classicist terms, a new Italian civilization finally liberated from the Goths, whose ascendancy, he believed, had paralleled the decline of the Roman Empire and Italy's descent into political and cultural chaos. Drawing inspiration from Trissino's classicist urban ideology, Palladio's early architectural designs include a classical facade for a series of city houses and a proposal for the Palazzo Civena—austere, simple, and thus repeatable prototypes, ready to be disseminated within the Gothic fabric of Vicenza.[5] The palazzo was fused with the more modest merchant house to form a new quasi-bourgeois *domus*. The centrality of the house and thus of secular domestic life, along with the systematic recovery of Roman architecture, provided the core of Palladio's attempt to define a universal formal grammar for the city.

But Palladio's first intellectual mentor was politically at odds with the Venetian republic. Trissino saw the fragmented city as a symptom of the larger political, cultural, and social fragmentation of the nation after the collapse of the Roman Empire. Like Dante in *De monarchia*, he called for a universal civic government, identifiable in Palladio's time with the singular figure of Holy Roman Emperor Charles V.[6] This universal government was to represent a new Roman Empire, a secular power free from both feudalism and ecclesiastical authority. Fundamental to these aspirations, the city and its architecture remained a key priority, and set against the Gothic fabric of the medieval city, Trissino promoted Roman architecture as the appropriate language for his political project.[7] Palladio made four research trips to Rome with Trissino as exercises in generating form through firsthand experience. The careful study of Roman antiquity was the express goal of this research, and the drawings Palladio made during these visits would become the source book of his architectural grammar. What is important to note here is Palladio's drawing method. Influenced by Raphael's recommendations about the depiction of ancient ruins, he avoided pictorial perspective and instead used a flat orthogonal technique that anticipated modern conventions of orthogonal projection—a method that contributed enormously to his systematic approach to the architecture of the city.[8] Architecture was not visionary and picturesque but scientific, the product of carefully defined rules. This fundamental distinction enabled the original form to be reconstructed out of the ruin, emancipating it from its reality as a fragment and giving it a new status as a component in a potential imperial city in Vicenza, and later across the Veneto.

Palladio's last trip to Rome in 1557 provided the material for two books, one of them a guide to the city's antiquities that would remain the standard reference for tourists for the next two centuries, the other a curious guide for pilgrims that documented Rome's many churches.[9] Whereas Roman antiquity offered the source for Palladio's universal architectural grammar, the mapping of churches—many of them located in typically suburban and depopulated, fragmented context—enabled him to present the city as an archipelago of monuments. These finite, autonomous artifacts carried a highly charged ritualistic geography, even when presented in isolation. But Palladio went beyond this by ordering the descriptions of the churches according to the pilgrim's peripatetic approach to the city. The guide does not describe these churches as monumental forms removed from their context, but addresses them within site-specific patterns of an urban itinerary. In addition to his study of antiquity, therefore, Palladio's interest in compiling a pilgrim's guide is of exceptional interest because it signifies his familiarity with the geographic symbolism of the city. And it is precisely this act of locating and marking that seems to underpin Palladio's ability to define the city through its architecture.

The heroic mission of Trissino and Palladio to recast Vicenza as a latter-day imperial city was prompted, somewhat more prosaically, by a fleeting celebration of religious authority: the entrance of Cardinal Ridolfi to the city in 1543. For this occasion, Palladio designed a sequence of temporary markers to delineate the cardinal's procession toward the cathedral. Two of the most exemplary urban landmarks of the Roman city—the triumphal arch and the obelisk—symbolized the veritable analogous Roman city generated by this circuit; Palladio considered them to be ideal and instant devices for urban reinvention, radically transforming the Gothic form of the city into a classical landscape.[10] The theme of the triumphal procession also highlights the city as a contested field of directions to be mapped and manipulated by a series of punctual interventions. Palladio's approach to the city, then, as his temporary installation for Vicenza makes clear, is based not on an overall urban plan but on the strong formal continuity and universalism evoked by his classical references. Yet, in contrast to the Roman city model, Palladio's universalism is defined by the concrete figure of architecture as a clearly circumscribed artifact, distinct from the ground of the city spaces surrounding it.

Palladio's mapping of Roman churches and his processional installation for Vicenza together anticipate his later mastery of the programming of architectural sequences. The variety of contexts in which he operated—the city of Vicenza, the Veneto countryside, and the Venetian Lagoon—offered an array of urban situations of various scales in which he could test the seamlessness of an architectural language against the inexorably fragmented nature of a city. The strategic link between the two extremes—continuity and discontinuity—is precisely the core dialectic of Palladio's urban design methodology.

In the sixteenth century Vicenza was one of Italy's most violent cities. Infighting among the most important families and political turmoil among the populace made it a theater of almost perpetual mayhem and murder.[11] The physical manifestations of this violence also unfolded within a larger conflict involving the local oligarchy, the colonial power of Venice, and the adversarial relationship between the church and the Veneto (at that time, Vicenza was the Italian epicenter of Calvinist and heretical sensibilities). Given this context, Trissino and Palladio's attempt to recast Vicenza as a model for an imperial city that evoked the *Pax*

Romana seems a very obvious and deliberate provocation—or, conversely, an attempt to use the unifying architectural language of classicism to project a self-harmonizing sense of civic calm. The grammar of this classicism lay in Palladio's impeccable use of the five orders as a way to make architecture intelligible as form, in contrast to the irrational patterns of the medieval city. There is an interesting parallel between Palladio's systematic use of the five orders and Trissino's political vision, based on the idea of a unifying secular government. Trissino (ever the poet and diplomat) was especially concerned with the reform of the Italian language, as evidenced by his letter to Pope Clement VII about the urgent need to address vernacular or colloquial Italian, and by his translation of Dante's *De vulgari eloquentia*. In many ways, Trissino's interest in the idea of grammar as a metahistorical political tool can be seen as the inspiration for Palladio's systematic approach to architecture, for Palladio used classicism not simply as a means of representation and authority but also as an ordered set of repeatable elements whose influence could extend beyond the construction of buildings to embrace the whole manifestation of the city itself. However, in order to be established, a grammar relies on clear examples. It is not by chance that Palladio's debut as an independent architect, under Trissino's mentorship, resulted in a design for the most important public monument in Vicenza: the completion of the Palazzo della Ragione, a vast civic hall built in the fifteenth century, and significantly renamed by Palladio as the "Basilica." Palladio's intervention was nothing more than a lintel-arch-lintel device, stacking two *serliane* orders built in white stone so that they wrapped the existing hall and shops underneath. The irregular structure of the existing building was absorbed by varying the length of the lintel without altering the arches. The building was thus conceived as a didactic display of the orders and their ability to support, correct, and mask the existing irregular Gothic structure. Moreover, his restructuring of the Basilica placed classicism at the heart of the civic space of the city as the hegemonic and universal architectural language of a long-desired *civitas*.

The Basilica, like many of Palladio's buildings, would not be completed during his lifetime. A permanent state of instability defined by wars, economic crises, disease, and, more spectacularly, the tormented vicissitudes of the families for whom Palladio worked, delayed or prevented their construction. It is easy to imagine that a desire to counteract this flux was the key impulse behind Palladio's *I quattro libri dell'architettura* (*The Four Books on Architecture*), which sets out all of his projects in order and according to his original design, regardless of alterations made during their construction. The four books, in this sense, suggest the emancipation of the idea of architecture from its material realization. Confronted with an unstable and complex environment, the language of building cannot tame the city in all its manifestations, but can only insert exemplary forms into its unstable body. As with his experiment for the triumphal route for Cardinal Ridolfi, Palladio's confidence in the city is revealed by the way he positions a building, even if he never proposed any ideal urban scheme. The architectural historian Franco Barbieri has suggested that although Palladio never predetermined the site of his projects, the location of his buildings seems to follow the Roman axial grid that was still legible in medieval Vicenza (it remains legible today—the intersection of a north-south *cardo* axis and an east-west *decumanus* is provided by the Corso Palladio and the route that goes from the ruins of the Roman Berga theater to the Pusterla bridge on the river Bacchiglione).[12] Trissino's utopian vision of Vicenza as a Roman city thus seems to be carried out in Palladio's insistence on this layout as the ordering principle of his interventions.

2.1
Andrea Palladio, Basilica, Vicenza, 1549 onward.
The classical orders "correct" the irregularities of
the preexisting Gothic structure of the Palazzo della
Ragione rather than masking them. The Basilica can
read as sublimating Trissino's political project of
universal government within the formal inner workings
of architectural form.

If we follow this hypothesis diachronically, we find along the *decumanus* the highly abstract forms of the Palazzo Chiericati (1550), the sophisticated facade of the Casa Cagollo (1559–1562), and the Palazzo Pojana (1560–1561). Nearby was the intended site of an unrealized project for the Palazzo Capra (1563–1564) and, at the end of the *decumanus*, directly opposite the Palazzo Chiericati, another Palazzo Capra. Following the perpendicular *cardo*, we start at the ruins of the Berga theater (itself a strategic precedent for Trissino and Palladio in their vision of resurrecting Vicenza's latent Roman plan) and then pass the bridge of San Paolo (which in the sixteenth century was believed to be another Roman structure), before arriving at the loggias of the Basilica and the Capitaniato at the intersection with the *decumanus*. The *cardo* would then lead us to two of Palladio's most impressive buildings—the Palazzo Montano Barbarano (1569–1570) and the Palazzo Porto (1549). Finally, we would end up at the Casa Bernardo Schio (1565–1566). Following the streets that run parallel to the *cardo*, toward the east we would find the Palazzo Da Monte (1541–1545), Palazzo Thiene (1542–1546), a project for a palazzo for Giacomo Angarano (1564), and a fragment of the Palazzo Pojana (1555). Similarly, following the streets that run parallel to the *decumanus*, on the north we would find projects for the Palazzo Trissino (1558) and a palazzo for Giambattista Garzadori, along with other minor but significant works such as Palladio's youthful interventions during his apprenticeship at the Pedemuro workshop with the church of Santa Maria in Foro (1531) and Vicenza's cathedral (1534–1536). Collectively, these interventions can be summarized as the mediation between two opposite forces which constitute the two major ingredients of all of Palladio's projects: on the one hand, an abstraction of the orders, proportion, and symmetry; and on the other, a site specificity, with each building being carefully inserted into the tight and complex medieval fabric of the city.

The project that most fully articulates this mediation is the Palazzo Chiericati. Strategically located on the edge of the Isola (the beginning of the *decumanus* and thus at the city gate approaching from Padua and Venice), the main facade of the palazzo consists of two superimposed loggias powerfully framed by the orders. But what is most striking about this design is that for the first time in the Renaissance the composition of the facade is rigorously projected into the interior. The elevation thus becomes a veritable index of the workings of the plan and section. At the same time, the space onto which this utopian architectural language is projected is far from ideal—the loggia is directly at odds with the narrow and long form of the site, derived in turn from the city's complex topography. Forcing the building to fit into its unlikely site generated an unprecedented compression in the plan, which reads as a kind of sixteenth-century barcode, with its sequence of compressed versions of atria, internal loggia, and a garden.[13] Moreover, within this logic, the facade's classical form may be understood as a clear political maneuver. Expanding the building's transverse section by only a few meters, the loggia occupies a portion of the Isola, not only creating a noble public gesture in one of the city's most important civic spaces, but also projecting a highly formal grammar. The generative principle of the building (the rule) and the peculiarities of the site (the exception) are thus intrinsically linked and mutually reinforced, producing a paradoxical combination of formal abstraction and radical site specificity.

It is precisely Palladio's mastering of the dialectic between continuity and discontinuity that theatrically emphasizes the urban role of his buildings as civic actors within Vicenza's analogous city—a dialectic also perfectly depicted by Canaletto in his own analogous city in the form of the painting he made of the Rialto Bridge. Rather than the actual bridge, Canaletto shows the bridge as designed by Palladio and presented in his *Quattro*

2.2
Antonio Canaletto, *Capriccio, or a Palladian Design for Rialto Bridge, with Buildings at Vicenza*, 1740s. In this painting, Canaletto depicts Palladio's project for an anti-ideal city made not by overall plans but by a coherent, yet disposable, architectural program. The scene depicts an imaginary view of Venice's Grand Canal with Palladio's unbuilt design for the Rialto Bridge framed by two buildings of Vicenza: the Basilica (right) and Palazzo Chiericati (left).

libri—a synthesis of two buildings, the Basilica and the Palazzo Chiericati, through a singularity of language and absolute forms. These forms are therefore precise in their paradigmatic integrity and yet disposable, to be used and combined according to the geography of the site.

More than his bridges and palazzos, however, the villas in the Veneto region are the most celebrated of Palladio's work. What is impressive about these buildings is not so much their architectural quality as their quantity. With the exception perhaps of Frank Lloyd Wright, no other architect has offered a portfolio filled with designs of such impressive continuity. The penchant for villas, a patrician typology of the Roman Empire, was revived in the fifteenth and sixteenth centuries.[14] In a rural economy, the villa's reappearance marked the transition from feudalism to the economic power of the estate. Fueled by this succession, Palladio assigned the villa a position of exceptional importance in his *Quattro libri*: five chapters of the second book are devoted to the architectural principles of this type, which is treated with the same attention to detail as other crucial city types such as palaces and religious buildings. By the time the *Quattro libri* was published, Palladio had already designed a large number of villas, and the serial nature of the solutions he developed (akin to the repeating rules he employed in his palaces in Vicenza and churches in Venice) had allowed him to define a consistent formal lexicon. Although made up of very few principles, this language was very strict in its application—notably, a clear symmetry of plan, an abundance of loggias in the form of belvederes and barns, the unconventional use of pediments, and the spatiality of imperial Roman baths (Palladio's most striking typological cross-contamination for rural buildings).

A number of historians have addressed Palladio's mixing of classical motifs, discussing his use of vernacular elements and his villa typology as providing both a country retreat and an economically and culturally productive rural hub. Much, too, has been written about his use of the pediment, which, but for one exception, had previously been confined to religious buildings (with the implied argument that temples and houses share the same origin).[15] Much less, however, has been said about how the interior space of Palladio's villas appropriated the spatiality of the imperial baths which he obsessively mapped, drew, and reconstructed during his field trips to Rome, and whose organization—a sequence of monumental spaces juxtaposed along axes of symmetry—lent his countryside villas a quintessentially metropolitan air. In many ways, the theatrical spatial complexity of the Roman bath offered an indoor miniaturized city. It is thus possible to speculate that Palladio's appropriation of the imperial bath and the pediment, and the conflation of these typologies with an agricultural context, are part of a strategy that goes beyond erudite references to Roman classicism and the accommodation of the material demands of the estate. Instead, it seems to have more to do with the idea of figuring the ground as an assemblage of metropolitan structures where the political and economic power of the Venetian archipelago (until then constituted by the sea) is projected analogically—that is, via the example of imperial Rome—toward the Veneto countryside. It is precisely this complex of analogical appropriations that made Palladio's architecture so successful and influential as an urban model.

Underlying all of Palladio's architectural output was the biggest crisis then facing the Serenissima Republic. Founded some time during the first decades of the eighth century and developed as a mercantile city-state, Venice's raison d'être had been economic transaction in the form of maritime commerce. Throughout its early history, this trade was bolstered not only by the city-state's

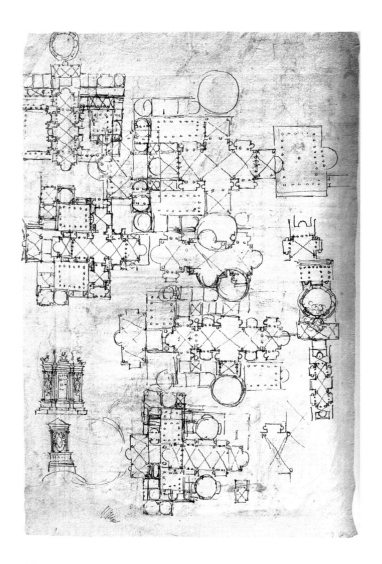

2.3
Andrea Palladio, study of the Baths of Agrippa
(with a detail of the Loggia del Capitaniato), 1570s.

geographical position at the edge of the Adriatic and the defeat
of other maritime republics such as Genoa, but also by the influence of the Byzantine Empire, which helped to establish Venice
as a privileged economic hub linking the Mediterranean basin
with commercial routes toward the east. However, Venice's im-
petuous rise came abruptly to an end with two major events. The
first was the War of the League of Cambrai (1508–1516), when
the most important European superpowers—Pope Julius II, Emperor Maximilian I, and King Louis XII of France—united against
the Serenissima in order to limit its land expansion. The second
decisive event, whose consequences would only slowly become
apparent over the course of the sixteenth century, was the discovery of the New World and the consequent shift of major maritime
traffic from east to west.

Confronted with this crisis, the Serenissima's oligarchy became convinced that they were about to enter a period of decline.
What is interesting about their response is that they accepted the
prospect of their diminishing fortune and, rather than seeking
to reverse what seemed inevitable, they did something politically
and conceptually far more radical: they attempted to slow down
the decline, so that instead of precipitating a sudden collapse,
the republic's waning influence could be tamed and governed as
a utopian condition of "duration."[16] Their response consisted of a
complex series of strategic maneuvers, all of them predicated on
a shift of Venice's economic basis from the sea to the land—from
maritime commerce to agriculture. Within this transfer, the
ground or *terra firma* suddenly took on the status of a territorial
project—one that included land reclamation, cartographic mapping, and the hydrological control of the network of rivers that
descended into Venice from high in the Alps.[17] And so, rather
than projecting itself solely toward the sea as a *stato del mar*,
Venice turned inward, toward its territorial lands—a (re)discov-

ery of its more earthly influence that must be seen as the defining context for Palladio's unprecedented succession of countryside villas, each commissioned by patricians of the Serenissma regime, and which would ultimately give Venice's project of duration its most enduring historical form.

Offering a kind of theoretical legitimacy to this shift from sea to land were the ideas of the theorist and patron of the arts Alvise Cornaro (1484–1566), who argued, in particular, for the promotion of agriculture as an alternative to Venice's existing mercantilist economy. Author of *La vita sobria*, a treatise on the virtue of living in the countryside, Cornaro was one of the most active political thinkers during the Veneto's economic crisis. His ideas largely concerned the reclamation of land and the promotion of agriculture over trade as the basis for a more solid relationship between power and territory.[18] Before Cornaro, country life (of which the villa was the most idealized form) was typically understood as radically antipolitical because it turned its back on the political space par excellence, the city. After Cornaro, however, this image was subverted. Rather than being predicated on the fundamentally apolitical ideas of disinterest and denial, the countryside became highly politicized by its promotion of a new formal model and its explicit rejection of the existing one—Venice. To represent his vision of civic life, Cornaro built his own analogous city near Padua, Palladio's birthplace. In the 1520s, he commissioned the Paduan painter Giovanni Battista Falconetto to produce a garden loggia, and a year later a stage was built next to it to host the performances of a famous local dialect actor, Angelo Beolco (better known by his pseudonym, Ruzzante). In Cornaro's garden it is possible to see an attempt to elevate the rustic countryside to the level of a new, cultivated civic condition—one that lay beyond the city's monumental spaces but had a competing measure of cultural and social charisma. Falconetto's loggia—the first example in the Veneto of architecture *alla romana*—was clearly built as a highly symbolic prototype, an example. Its key feature is the formal theme of the loggia itself, with its generous openings, didactic exposition of the orders as a new lingua franca of civic life, and theatrical framing of the garden, which made the loggia both the scenery and the spectators' tribune. This compositional dialectic between subject and object, between a point of view and a space framed within it, would be the basis of Palladio's own unique approach to landscape. In all of his work, the encircling territory is not a passive ground waiting to be activated by the imposition of a figure, but a specific site made of existing natural and artificial elements of which the object—the villa—becomes a theatrical frame. In this sense, Palladio's villas are not simply objects enclosed within a reconstructed context (like the Medici villas in the Florentine hills or Pirro Ligorio's Villa d'Este), but are specific objects that frame and redefine the existing landscape as an economic, cultural, and political counter to the city.

The Villa Emo in Fanzolo (1556) perhaps best shows the radicalism of Palladio's approach to the relationship between the villa and its immediate landscape. It is his simplest and most obviously minimal villa, and yet its structure, like all the others, is based on the clear juxtaposition of the *casa dominicale* (palace) with the flanking *barchesse*, which served as storage and as a covered gallery passage between the central body and the symmetrical *colombare* along its two sides. Unlike his other villas, however, this juxtaposition is revealed along the same frontal plane, a device that accentuates the Villa Emo's perpendicularity against the horizontality of the surrounding Veneto plains. In its simplicity, the villa heightens the importance of directing the landscape, not by imposing on it a new, meticulously regulated ground arrangement, but by figuring it through the simple act of

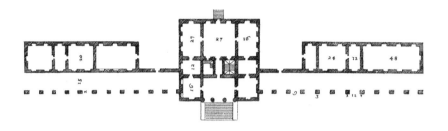

2.4
Andrea Palladio, plan and facade of Villa Emo
(1555–1565), as engraved in the *Quattro libri
dell'architettura* (1570).

framing. Palladio does this by developing one side of the villa as a continuous row of loggias and the other side as a row of windows, thereby establishing, in a very powerful way, the experience of front and back within the vastness of the building's landscape.

With the Villa Emo we see the classic Palladian paradox of a building that has been designed according to its own compositional logic (typically based on symmetry), yet at the same time is also inflected so as to react to its specific site condition. This paradox is further radicalized in Palladio's most famous (and most bizarre) building, the Villa Capra, or La Rotonda (1567). In the *Quattro libri*, this villa is included in the section dedicated to urban palaces, an aspirational characterization that further reveals Palladio's attempt to transform a building in the countryside into a veritable civic form.[19]

Palladio's equation of city and countryside is already visible in the very obvious formal similarities between his rural villas and civic palaces (apart from the absence of the barns, the palaces are the same as the villas—for example, the Palazzo Antolini in Udine bears a striking similarity to the Villa Pisani in Montagnana). And yet at the Rotonda, the unity of city and countryside is further radicalized, as if the building were a kind of manifesto. Situated on a hilltop just outside Vicenza, the villa was clearly designed as an ideal "observatory" of the landscape (a conceptual and iconoclastic program revealed by the long description of the site that prefaces this project in the *Quattro libri*). The vastness and variety of this landscape is exemplified in the form and peculiar composition of the villa itself: it is a rather small building with four huge porticos made up of colonnades, pediments, and ramps. As is well documented, this unusual form for a house was inspired by the temple at the top of the Sanctuary of Fortuna Primigenia in Palestrina, a building Palladio had visited while in Rome. Yet with the Rotonda, the monumentality and depth of the villa's porticos appear exaggerated against the scale of the actual building—a contrast that suggests that rather than being grand entranceways into the villa, they are actually oriented outward, toward the surrounding countryside. Thus, the porticos act more like theaters for a spectacle that predates the building: the landscape all around. If we follow this reading, then the classical view of Palladio's Rotonda as a pyramidal composition in which the building forms the pinnacle of the hill is subverted, if not inverted: the diagram of the villa is not about a conventional architectural relationship in which the outside is drawn toward the inside but is a relationship in which the inside is always projecting outward. The formal symmetry of the building is thus an index of the Rotonda's territorial site specificity. Moreover, the fact that the building's symmetry required all four sides to have a portico, and Palladio's placement of a dome over them (the first time such a detail was used in a residential building), convey not a unidirectional aspect but a roundness that suggests an analogy with the infinity of the landscape outside. The result is that the Rotonda subverts both architectural convention, with its inversion of the dominance of the building over its site, and the conventions of Renaissance drama and the rigidities of proscenium front-to-back projection. Fundamentally, then, the building is as radical theatrically as it is architecturally.

Ultimately, and to a certain extent, naturally, it was in Venice that Palladio finally seemed able to satisfy his project of the city. His buildings constructed there, which are mostly churches, can all be seen against the backdrop of Venice's economic, geographic, and political crises, but more immediately they relate to two significant proposals for restructuring and preserving the city in the wake of the Serenissima's demise. The first was a project initiated by Cristoforo Sabbadino (1489–1543), Venice's first and most illustrious hydraulic engineer, who began to develop the city's borders in the form of a ring of waterfront *fondamenta*—large embankments that would enclose and define Venice's *forma urbis*. (The Fondamenta Nuove and Fondamenta Zattere, two of the city's most suggestive sites, still visible today, were the result of this proposal.) Sabbadino envisioned this ring not only as a functional element and a necessary limit to the city, but as a new monumental space that, if realized in its entirety, would have opened up the city toward the vastness of the Lagoon.[20]

The second visionary project, culturally more complex and sophisticated, was an elaboration by Alvise Cornaro of the concept of the theater he had constructed in his garden in Padua. Like Sabbadino, Cornaro aimed to synthesize two apparently contradictory forces by opening the city toward the Lagoon while at the same time insisting on a clearly defined urban edge. The project itself was articulated in two parts. The first consisted of a man-made grove of trees planted on a linear island, built in the form of a floating city wall. Besides being proposed as a defense system, offering protection from military attacks and the forces of the sea, this wooded isthmus would also have served as social infrastructure for the city—in effect, a gigantic park. The project's second part focused on the most strategic and monumental point in the city: the basin of San Marco, the vast and monumental space triangulated by the Piazzetta of San Marco, the Punta della Dogana, and the island of San Giorgio Maggiore. Within this space Cornaro imagined another triangulation—a floating theater *alla romana*: an artificial island in the form of a "shapeless little hill," built out of the mud extracted from the city's canals, planted with trees and topped with a loggia; and a spring-water fountain set on the edge of the piazzetta, right between the two monumental columns featuring Venice's twin patrons, the lion of St. Mark and the statue of San Teodoro of Amasea, which framed the view of the basin from St. Mark's

Square. The rationale for this composition (and, as Manfredo Tafuri has noted, its powerful ideological resonances)[21] seems to have been to introduce a territorial condition into Venice's largely aquatic universe. Yet what is interesting about this insertion is that it is formalized not by destroying Venice's insularity, but by theatrically emphasizing the silhouette of the Lagoon as an archipelago.

The schemes of both Sabbadino and Cornaro were designed to expand the city beyond the limits of its traditional monumental spaces, which until then had been iconographically controlled by the Piazza San Marco. Elements of Cornaro's urban vision—notably the freshwater spring and the linear wooded glade—were also clearly meant to introduce, analogically, the theme of agriculture and land management into a city that had previously developed only through its maritime economy. Moreover, the island theater, imagined as a place of public spectacle and thus, like the archipelago of trees, conceived as a piece of social infrastructure, emphasized the performative character of the entire project. Within the context of the Serenissima Republic, the theater was the most popular formal register of a kind of intrinsic, collective art of memory, which made it the most effective formal typology for staging broader political and cultural ideas. Significantly, Cornaro's theater on water was imagined according to the precepts of Vitruvius's ancient Roman theater as reconstructed by Daniele Barbaro in his 1556 edition of *De architectura*—an edition illustrated by Palladio. Thus, an island (Venice's defining urban form) in the shape of a theater (the classical type par excellence) offered the centerpiece of Cornaro's territorial project for Venice, and made explicit precisely what was also at the core of Palladio's analogical language: the utopian and timeless abstraction of architecture, and its ability to evoke potential or even pregnant geographic and political scenarios. The difference between

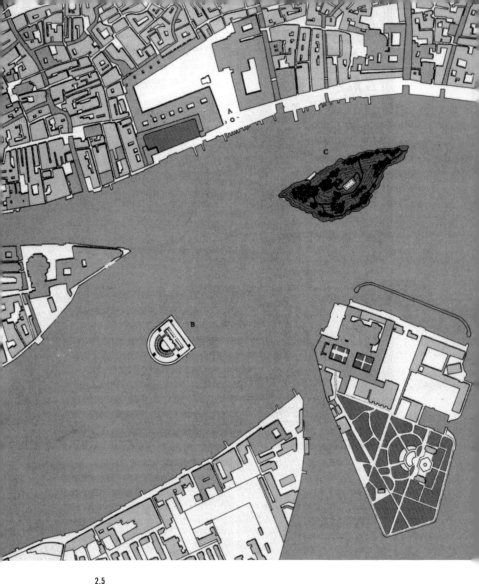

2.5
Graphic reconstruction of Alvise Cornaro's project
for the Basin of San Marco: (A) the fountain; (B) the
theater; (C) the "shapeless little hill." (Drawing by
Luca Ortelli, from Manfredo Tafuri, *Venice and the
Renaissance*, fig. 115.)

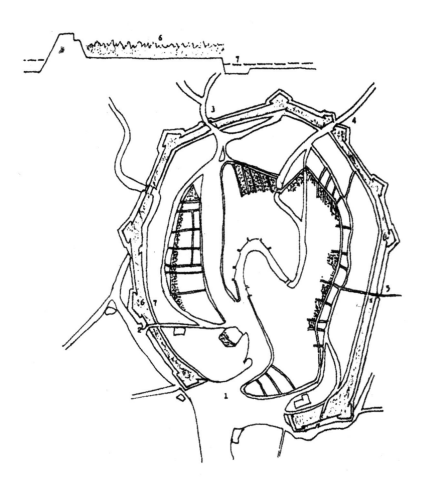

2.6
Reconstruction of Venice surrounded by walls in the
Lagoon according to Cornaro. (From Manfredo Tafuri,
Venice and the Renaissance, fig. 117.)

Sabbadino's urban project and Cornaro's vision is that while Sabbadino aimed at the consolidation of the existing city, Cornaro imagined a new Venice that radically invested architecture by stressing the analogy between the singularity of the architectural artifact and the insularity of the city form.

Both projects, however, were united in introducing an urban theme that is key to Palladio's monumental interventions in Venice: the idea of the urban edge not just as city form but also as a new monumental space linking the city to its territorial context—in this case, the Lagoon. In other words, there is a link between the idea of the edge, as introduced by the projects of both Sabbadino and Cornaro, and the physical location of all of Palladio's Venetian buildings. Of course, Palladio never actively chose the site for any of these projects (the site always came with the commission), but in retrospect it is impossible not to see that nearly all of his interventions in Venice were situated on the edge of the city—for example, the facade for San Pietro di Castello (1559), the facade of the church of San Francesco alla Vigna (1564–1565), the church and monastery of San Giorgio Maggiore (1560–1565), the church of the Redentore (1592), and the church and hospice of the Zitelle (1574). Besides their occupation of the periphery, all of these projects also share the same formal language and, above all, a common lexicon for the facade: an austere and hieratic classicism made of the rigorous use of the orders; the superimposition of facades (a technique invented by Palladio but clearly inspired by Bramante as well as by Vitruvius's description of the Fano basilica); and, most obviously, the unprecedented use of *pietra d'Istria*, a white stone that renders the buildings in marked contrast to the vernacular brick, plaster, and wood colors of the city. Visually pronounced, then, not simply by their removal to the edge of the city but also by their striking white stone elevations, Palladio's churches—in particular San Giorgio Maggiore, Redentore, and Zitelle—also radiated their difference through their foreground, the open Giudecca canal or basin. If the palaces in Vicenza are still flanked by the existing medieval fabric, and the villas across the Veneto are mediated by vernacular elements such as the *barchesse*, it is only in Venice—through the wide open expansiveness of the Venetian Lagoon and the loaded, neither-sea-nor-land archetype of the archipelago—that Palladio was able to establish his architecture as an absolute geopolitical form.

In the end, in order to fully understand Palladio's analogical Venice, we need to go back to his earliest failed assault on the city and the first of two proposals he made for a new Rialto Bridge (1556). In this project Palladio programmatically established an approach to the city that is anything but classical. The bridge—a central theme of Roman urbanism where infrastructure and monument are indissolubly linked—is conceived here as a civic hub made up of two parallel rows of shops spanning the Grand Canal. On either side, two identical, gigantic squares frame the approaches to the bridge, enclosed by an uninterrupted columned gallery. Though only ever illustrated in plan, the form of this project is impressive. And, as with everything Palladio produced, it should be seen not *in vacuo* but in relation to the tight and intricate Gothic fabric of the city— as absolute space miraculously emerging out of the existing dark, labyrinthine city structure.

In the second version of the project—the one published in the *Quattro libri* and painted by Canaletto—Palladio focused only on the bridge. At its center he placed a classical square flanked by two symmetrical colonnaded galleries that would host the various shops. By moving the theme of the city square from the entrances to the center of the span, Palladio transformed the bridge into a forum, a microcosm dialectically linked to the city by virtue of its radical autonomy as a city within the city.

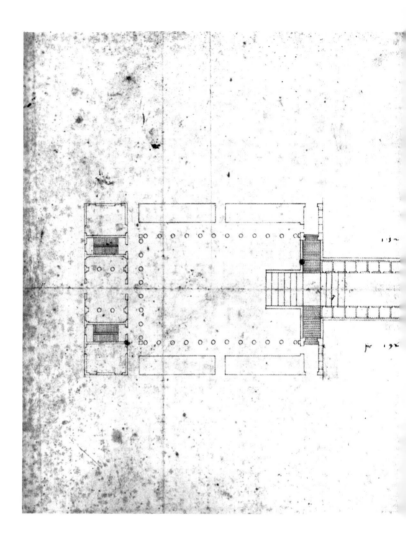

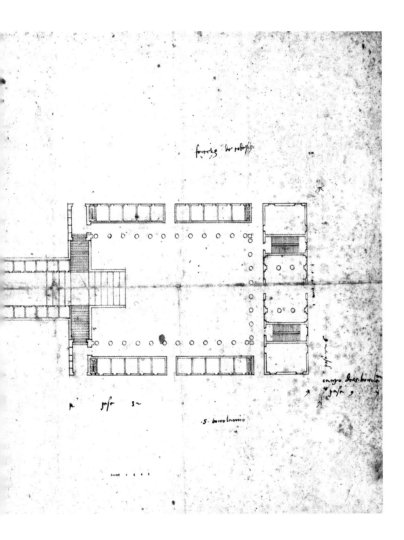

2.7
Andrea Palladio, first design for the Rialto Bridge,
1551–1554. The rigid geometric form of this scheme
evokes *per via negativa* the topographic intricacy of
the context.

The analogical motive of the Rialto Bridge—as Tafuri once noted—is the radical contrast that Palladio established between the static, somewhat sober character of the forum/square (the elevation of which was designed in the form of a temple, topped by a pediment) and the everyday hustle and bustle of the canal activities below—a contrast perfectly captured in Canaletto's painting. According to this analogy, Palladio's bridge acts as a frame for Venice's constituent elements—a "mental montage," as Tafuri describes it—that defines Palladio's approach to the city.[22] Tafuri argues that "the utopian character of the Rialto project seems to have been generated by a design principle that transformed the city into a territory. In this city-territory the heroic image of architecture entered the city in the form of finite parts, of points that defined the city, without reducing it to an all-encompassed form."[23]

It is precisely this characteristically modern dialectic between the absoluteness of architecture and the openness of the city that Palladio's unique architectural approach sought to establish. Using forms and typologies to effect contextual relationships and political visions, he fundamentally reimagined not only the physical manifestation of the city but its very idea. Significantly, however, unlike most other key theorists of architecture—such as Vitruvius, Alberti, Filarete, or Serlio—Palladio never produced a comprehensive theory or plan, or even a general view of the city. Even though his architecture takes the form of repeatable prototypes, his projects are always rigorously site-specific. As a result, Palladio did not take part in one of the topics through which architectural culture in the fifteenth and sixteenth centuries is repeatedly defined—the "ideal city."

In the popular imagination, ideal cities are those rationally planned, perfectly harmonious Renaissance municipalities whose structure and image reflected the rediscovery of humanist

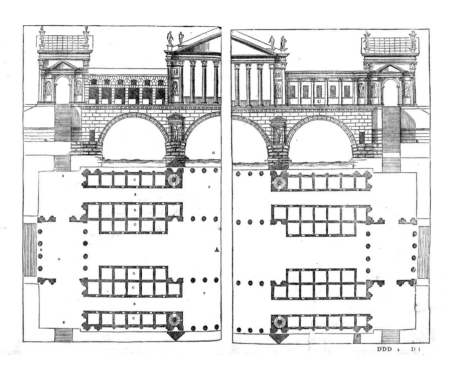

DDD 2   D 1

2.8
Andrea Palladio, "Stone bridge of my own invention,"
design for the Rialto Bridge as engraved in the *Quattro libri
dell'architettura* (1570). The image of the temple contrasts
with the hectic life of the Grand Canal. The project shows
Palladio's dialectical montage of forms at its best.

values within a culture of civic coexistence. But in order to effectively understand how the radicalism of Palladio's project for the city subverted this image, we need to go beyond its conventional interpretation. What is traditionally referred to as an "ideal city" is in fact a complex of theories, projects, and actions for a city designed according to rational and scientifically intelligible criteria. Its origin dates back to Greco-Roman times and the founding of *ex novo* settlements according to repeatable principles independent from the context in which they were to be applied. These principles, often under the umbrella of a singular urban layout, aimed to more effectively link the internal social management of a city with its defense against outside enemy forces. Mediating between the ancient Greek *oikos* (household) and *polis* (city-state), the idealism of the city therefore incorporated everything from the private space of the family house to the militarization of the city-state.[24]

With the fall of the Roman Empire in 476 CE, however, a paralysis ensued in the evolution of the European city that lasted through the eleventh century, as settlements took the form of small, self-sufficient citadels or fortress cities—practically diagrams of the politics of feudalism. The feudal model, of course, proved to be as economically unsustainable as it was architecturally unnavigable, and it was against this model that the city as *civitas* was rediscovered as the fundamental structure for human coexistence from the fourteenth century onward. It is precisely this rediscovery—together with the recovery of the juridical implications of being a citizen as opposed to a feudal *subditus*—that prompted philosophers and, later, architects to retrace the legacy of antiquity as a model for the new city. Vitruvius's *De architectura*, rediscovered in the fifteenth century, was an emblem of this historicism, and supported not only an erudite antiquarianism but also a treatise on city management covering all scales of the urban project from the design of houses to warfare.

It was in this context that figures such as Alberti, Francesco di Giorgio, and Filarete expanded the task of the architect from designing buildings to designing entire cities. Subsequently, the image of the ideal city as orderly and conceived according to a rational plan appears in many fifteenth-century paintings, precisely reflecting the political immediacy of urban design. Here the Renaissance invention of perspective clearly resonates, because it demonstrated the possibility of reducing the space of the city to the manageable logic of calculation and the mapping and organization of spatial and geographical facts. But for all the perspectival idealism exemplified by architects like Sebastiano Serlio, Italy in the fifteenth and sixteenth centuries was in reality so politically fragmented and unstable that an overall planning of its cities according to rational criteria was quite impossible. Those Italian cities that do appear as "ideal" (towns like Pienza in Tuscany or Vigevano in Lombardy) are in fact fairly restricted spaces enveloped by a medieval urban fabric. Interestingly, this is also the case with Rome, a city long predicated on a chaotic and somewhat haphazard model of urban growth. Although the city's papacy in the fifteenth and sixteenth centuries attempted to reconstruct Rome in accordance with its ancient splendor, such plans materialized only in the form of small interventions within the existing infrastructure. For example, Bramante's implementation of Pope Julius II's vision for Rome as an imperial city was (partially) realized, not in the form of an overall plan, but as a strategic positioning of large-scale architectural artifacts connected by an axial grid of roads. Given the limited scope of these interventions, architects like Bramante tended to overload the metonymical and microcosmic resonances of individual buildings in an architectural organism whose formal and spatial composition (via the use of porticos, squares, forums, villas, and basilicas) exuded the exemplary characteristics of ancient cities. Consider, for example, his Belvedere in the Vatican, where the model of an ancient villa—with explicit references to the Sanctuary of Fortuna Primigenia in Palestrina—is translated into a massive, self-contained courtyard building. Through overly symbolic structures like these, Renaissance Italy's project for the city shifted away from the overall plan à la Filarete toward analogical representations based around contained, finite architectural compositions.

Palladio, like Bramante, looked to the ancient monuments of Rome not simply as sources for the correct interpretation of the orders, but as complex organisms that reproduced the rich architectural qualities of a city. It was for this reason that he so carefully studied the model of the Roman bath, an urban type to which he had planned to devote one whole book in his unfinished architectural treatise. Palladio viewed the bathhouse as a unique public structure because, unlike temples or basilicas, it grouped together multiple programs and activities, lending it an intricacy through its sequence of different spaces. This same spatiality is often evoked in Palladio's villas, palaces, and churches. Think, for example, of the interiors of the Redentore or San Giorgio Maggiore, the forms of which are the result of radically different spatial models, each developed according to its own autonomous geometries and linked together only by the symmetry and continuity of the orders. Or consider the two extraordinary projects for palaces in Venice, published in the second book, whose plans develop around the elucidation of a succession of spaces, the sequence of which is not simply reducible to the traditional tripartite Renaissance palazzo atrium or courtyard.[25]

The same miniaturization of city space into compound architectural artifacts also pushed Palladio to reconstruct Greek and

Latin squares (following Vitruvius's description) in the *Quattro libri*, as models for a variety of colonnaded indoor and outdoor spaces. Because they were associated with the forums of ancient Rome, porticos made by colonnades became the definitive architectural response in framing open, public civic space. Within this analogical context, as we have seen in the Palazzo Chiericati, the Basilica, or the Palazzo Civena, Palladio would often introduce a ground-floor portico, thereby instantly transforming the building from a simple, self-standing object to an entity that symbolically resonated with all of the formal attributes of the city around it. By incorporating public spaces, these buildings were not simply outstanding examples of architecture, but exemplars of an architectural relationship to the city. It is this explicit will to idealize that made Palladio's collective series of buildings the absolute embodiment of a project for the city. Yet the impact of these examples should not be viewed simply in terms of their role in establishing an architectural pattern book (a subservience to type and form that has made Palladio one of the most copied architects in the history of the discipline). Instead, Palladio's portfolio is more powerfully influential within a cultural understanding of the Renaissance city, offering specific architectural compositions that immediately evoke paradigms of city space.

As Giorgio Agamben has written, the act of making an example is a complex business because it presupposes that in order to represent the canon, an example has to be conceptually disconnected from the forms of its everyday use.[26] In the rhetorical mechanisms of an example, form is not simply an object in itself but an object that operates as a paradigm for something else. Agamben also reminds us that in Latin culture there was a distinction between an exemplar, something to be appreciated and understood only with the senses—and thus something destined to be imitated—and an exemplum, a form whose interpretation requires additional intellectual or symbolic references.

It is exactly as an exemplum that Palladio's architecture operates, with its subtle references to ancient typologies and resonances to wider geographical and political contexts. Through Palladio, architecture extends its influence on the city precisely by being a finite and thus clearly recognizable thing, a "species"—in the sense that the Marxist philosopher Paolo Virno has used the term—consisting of a sole individual that can only be politically reproduced and never be transposed into an omnivorous general program.[27] The power of the exemplum resides in its ability to propose a general paradigmatic framework rather than a set of regulations or commands to be literally deployed. As an exemplum, Palladio's architectural form is not deployed onto a plan, nor is it an urban rule; rather, it is invested with the representation of an alternative idea of the city within the very space of the existing city.

Such an intuitively tactical understating of architecture, as both a coherent set of principles and a mobile element never tied to an overall plan, seems to have its origin in Palladio's passion for the art of war.[28] In the *Quattro libri* he notes that the imperative to construct perimeter walls is of little use to the successful defense of a city compared to the training of the soldiers and an accurate knowledge of the surrounding territory—thus demonstrating a militarized understanding of landscape and civic management which was also faithfully represented in his battle illustrations for the sixteenth-century publication of Polybius's *Histories*. What is interesting about these troop formation diagrams is the way they replicate his villas' own framing of the landscape. This mentality, which fused the stability of architecture with the fluid complexity of new urban spaces and forms, seems to have made Palladio deeply skeptical about any overarching urban plan, and pushed him instead to frame his (implicit) project for the city in the same way he understood the art of war—as a project tactically open to the multiplicity of its territorial circumstances and yet resolute in its formal strategy. In this respect, Palladio's accessible geography of architectures can be read as exemplars of a city no longer constrained by its walled *civitas*, but as a territory whose form lies in its attempt to trace and make explicit the geographical and political conditions of its existence.

3 INSTAURATIO URBIS
PIRANESI'S *CAMPO MARZIO* VERSUS NOLLI'S
NUOVA PIANTA DI ROMA

Within the history of projects for cities, no image for a "new city" is as radical as the *Scenographia Campi Martii*, engraved by Giovanni Battista Piranesi as the prologue to the Venetian architect's more famous plate, the *Ichnographia Campi Martii antiquae urbis*, an eighteenth-century "reconstruction" of Rome in the age of the Roman Empire. In the *Scenographia*, Piranesi presents an image of Rome in which several existing ruins from its imperial past stand in a desolate landscape. Representing neither the existing city nor the ancient city, this engraving simply depicts the few surviving ruins of Piranesi's day, minus the context of modern Rome: the ruins are not restored but are represented in their current condition, as if they had been liberated from all subsequent historical layers. Here the ruins can be read both as what had survived the subsequent development of the city and as the conceptual guides for the reconstruction of a new city, which Piranesi would present in the *Ichnographia* plate. His *Scenographia* thus condenses three seemingly conflicting actions—destruction, restoration, and reconstruction of the city—into one representation. To understand the ideological purpose of such a project, it is necessary to situate the *Campo Marzio* and its source, Piranesi's radical mapping of Rome in *Le antichità romane*, within the important tradition

3.1
Giovanni Battista Piranesi, *Scenographia Campi Martii*,
from *Il Campo Marzio dell'antica Roma* (1762). The
modern city has been removed. Once fragments of a past
civilization, new ruins are the beginning of a "new" city.

3.2
Giovanni Battista Piranesi, *Ichnographia
Campi Martii antiquae urbis*, 1762.

of *instauratio urbis*: the attempts to restore the form of ancient Rome, beginning in the fifteenth century.[1] The representational logic of Piranesi's *Scenographia* was inspired by Flaminio Nardini's image of the Campo Marzio in his book *Roma antica* (Piranesi's favorite reconstruction of ancient Rome) and by Bonaventura van Overbeke's plan of ancient Rome.[2] Both maps depict Rome as constituted by only a few select monuments or ruins, with the city itself removed. This representation of Rome was common in many attempts to represent the form of the city beginning in the Middle Ages: the Limbourg Brothers, Taddeo di Bartolo, and Fazio degli Uberti, for example, each mapped Rome as a city seemingly set in a desert punctuated by a few singular architectural artifacts.[3] These depictions had their roots in the *Mirabilia urbis Romae*, the first guidebook to introduce religious pilgrims and visitors to the ruins of Rome.

After the fall of the Roman Empire, the city contracted in size to the area of the Campo Marzio along the bend of the Tiber River. Most of the ancient *mirabilia*, or "marvels"—the baths, the triumphal arches, and even major Christian basilicas—in the eastern part of the city were abandoned. For centuries the ruins of these monuments were depicted as objects floating in open fields. This situation was still visible, for example, in Leonardo Bufalini's map of Rome, engraved in 1551, which Giovanni Battista Nolli redrew to serve as an appendix to his *Nuova pianta di Roma* in 1748. In the redrawn Bufalini map, the *intra muros* city consists of two parts: on the left, framed by the bend of the Tiber, is the modern city, which Nolli represents as an extensive built mass patterned by an intricate web of streets, retaining the few axes built between the fifteenth and sixteenth centuries and punctuated by several monuments; on the right, the large complexes of ancient Rome are like islands adrift in a landscape of hills. The map depicts a dialectical city whose form is made by the juxtaposition of two

3.3
Bonaventura van Overbeke, *Roma antica*, 1708.

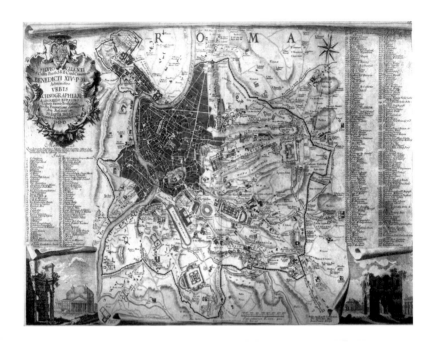

3.4
Giovanni Battista Nolli, rendition of Leonardo
Bufalini's 1551 map of Rome, 1748.

conditions: the modern city, with its figure-ground relationship between monuments and the organic fabric of the city, and the ancient city, with its monuments completely liberated from their urban framework. This urban composition is unique. It dramatically reveals the difference between the inhabited city, with its urban framework of streets and squares, and the deserted city, whose potential is open to multiple possibilities.

In comparison, in the *Campo Marzio*, Piranesi displaces the urban fabric that for centuries characterized the eastern part of the city to the site of the modern city: the Campo Marzio. In the *Scenographia*, he envisions the destruction of modern Rome as a precondition for a new Rome, designed through the restoration of its ancient form. The link between these two Romes is the few extant ruins, which Piranesi selected for the introduction to his topographical reconstruction of the Campo Marzio.

In ancient Rome, the Campo Marzio was a chaotic agglomeration of large architectural complexes. Unlike the originary sites in Rome's landscape of hills, the Campo Marzio was a flat area subject to recurring flooding of the Tiber. As a result, it was populated mostly by public buildings such as theaters and circuses, but like the rest of Rome the Campo Marzio had developed without a plan; the area was defined simply by the juxtaposition of its buildings. After the fall of the Roman Empire, the ruins of these complexes were absorbed by the first nucleus of medieval Rome. Ruins were used as the foundations for new buildings, resulting in an intricate pattern of streets that evolved from the chaotic condition of the area. Piranesi's *Campo Marzio* was an attempt to reconstruct the ancient form of this part of the city, but his representation of the project was more than just a visionary archaeological reconstruction. Indeed, the *Campo Marzio* can be understood as a project for the city that Piranesi composed as a polemical response to the condition of Rome in his time.

Much has been written on Piranesi's project, but it is not fair to judge its topographical and architectural inventiveness as utopia or, worse, as an architectural fantasy. Rather, Piranesi's *Campo Marzio* can be considered the summa of a vision of the city that developed between the fifteenth and eighteenth centuries: *instauratio urbis*, which literally means "the installment of the city," and in practice involved the reconstruction of the ancient form of the city. Rather than being simply antiquarian or erudite exercises, these reconstructions were attempts to restore the latent vocation of the city: Rome as capital not only of the ancient world but also of the modern world.

Because ancient Rome had no overall plan, the restoration advanced by *instauratio urbis* took the form of a careful and selective topographic survey of the ancient ruins of the city. It is important to emphasize that the implicit project of many *instaurationes urbis* was the liberation of the ancient ruins from the modern city that had developed around them. Unlike the earlier *Mirabilia* tradition, in *instauratio urbis* ruins were no longer seen as the remnants of a past world, nor as mere melancholic mementos of the greatness of ancient Rome. Instead, *instauratio urbis* used the remnants of the ancient city as clues for the reconstruction of a new Rome. One of the most important proponents of this project was the artist Raphael, whose ideas to protect and restore the ruins of ancient Rome were presented to Pope Leo X by Baldassarre Castiglione. This proposal to preserve antiquity was one of the earliest examples of a desire for an urban project focused on the concept of heritage.[4]

One of the most impressive attempts at *instauratio urbis* is Pirro Ligorio's *Antiquae urbis imago* of 1561.[5] Ligorio's process of cross-referencing antiquarian findings exemplified the method that was typical of *instauratio urbis*, in which ruins were not just evidence of a past per se, but also became examples that resonated conceptually and formally as the foundations for the grammar of contemporary city forms. Ligorio selected evidence from ruins, from schematic images of ancient buildings as represented on coins, and from references in ancient literature, and then formed a coherent architectural grammar through which he was able to reconstruct the entirety of the city's architecture. Ligorio's reconstruction of ancient Rome is the most direct precedent for Piranesi's *Campo Marzio*.[6] In Ligorio's *Imago*, Rome appears as a city almost without streets and crowned by objects: different compositions of domes, pyramids, pitched roofs, obelisks, amphitheaters, exedras, porticos, and circuses. The *Imago* is the most radical representation of a city whose form is embodied in the composition of its buildings rather than dictated by an overall plan. When Le Corbusier discussed Rome as a city composed of architectural forms "against the illusion of the plan," it was not by chance that he traced a detail of Ligorio's *Imago*.[7] With this example, Le Corbusier argued that, against the pretensions of urban axiality and overall city plans, the "Lesson of Rome" proposed a city form made by the juxtaposition of the sheer mass and volumes of its monumental buildings.[8]

Because ancient Rome was an accumulation of individual complexes without an overall plan, any attempt at *instauratio urbis* began with the careful topographic siting of the ancient ruins. The city had to be mapped ruin by ruin in a never-ending adventure of antiquarian and topographical exploration. For the architects who were reconstructing Rome, *instauratio urbis* meant adherence to a city form that was not reducible to a single overall logic, but that revealed itself through the city's individual architectures and their relationship with the surrounding geography. In this thinking, *instauratio urbis* was an infinite puzzle: every time something was discovered, mapped, and reconstructed, an ensuing enquiry on ancient Rome would contest the discovery and propose an alternative reconstruction.

3.5
Pirro Ligorio, *Antiquae urbis imago*, 1561
(detail of the central area of the city).

What sort of intellectual and conceptual impetus sustained this reconstruction of antiquity, of which Piranesi's *Campo Marzio* is the ultimate realization? What was at stake in this endless attempt to trace the ancient form of Rome? In short, why did the ancient form become such a topical drive in the development of the city for at least three centuries?

As seen in Palladio's survey of Rome, interest in ancient ruins was motivated not by an abstract respect for heritage but rather by its political instrumentality, which often coincided with the desire to refound and reconstruct the city. The motivation of *instauratio urbis* also reveals the ideological ground zero for the revival of antiquity during what, since the nineteenth century, has been called the Renaissance.

The ideology of *instauratio urbis* originated in the political awakening of the Roman *populus* in the fourteenth century, after a long period of political and social backwardness that had afflicted the city since the fall of the Roman Empire. A decisive event in this awakening was the revolt of the people of Rome, led by Cola di Rienzo, against the aristocratic rulers left in power by the absence of the popes. As Manfredo Tafuri has noted, Cola's uprising was not simply a revolt but a truly "cultural revolution," the effects of which reverberated through Rome for centuries.[9] Its ideological trigger was rooted in the first attempt to reevaluate the cultural legacy of ancient Rome as a counterweight to the feudal power of the fourteenth-century city's ruling families. The uprising was legitimated by the discovery of the *Lex romana*, written on bronze tablets at the time of the Emperor Vespasian, which Cola symbolically inserted in the apse of the church of San Giovanni, the cathedral of Rome, with theatrical ceremony.[10] According to the *Lex romana*, it was the *populus* who had conceded power to the emperor. This finding had explosive ramifications, because it made clear that the power of the ruler of Rome and his

rendering of many infrastructures focuses more on their materiality than on their function. This is evident in *Le rovine del castello dell'Acqua Giulia*, his survey of the waterworks that managed the flow coming from what Piranesi believed to be the Aqua Julia. In the survey presentation, Piranesi counterposes details of the *castello*'s function with views of the ruin itself. The massive presence of the ruin, its form consumed by nature, takes precedence over the image of its function. In contrast to the continuity and connectedness that is implicit in infrastructure when viewed topographically (as in Nolli), Piranesi offers close-ups of the physical attributes of the waterworks as finite forms. Such a presentation emancipates these elements from their role in an encompassing system and depicts them as autonomous forms.

Discontinuity is also emphasized as a spatial attribute of the city. Increasing the dimensions of elements is a constant technique in Piranesi's views of Rome. Beginning with his early *vedute*, Piranesi took the opposite approach from Vasi. Whereas Vasi recorded the landscape of Rome with a realism that accurately depicts elements within balanced scenes, thus manifesting a desire to mollify the formal and political impetus that animated the development of Rome, Piranesi alters the scenes of baroque Rome in order to increase both the proportions of the architecture and the dimensions of the space in between buildings. For example, in his views of modern Rome, which Piranesi executed throughout his life in order to finance his antiquarian projects, he deliberately changed the scale of the city by enlarging the narrow spaces between monuments. We can see this in the small *vedute*, where the monumental buildings of the Renaissance and baroque Rome, such as the Palazzo della Cancelleria, Palazzo di Propaganda Fide, Palazzo Borghese, and Archiginnasio della Sapienza, sometimes appear as completely isolated masses, when in reality these buildings were often part of the baroque

3.17
Giovanni Battista Piranesi, view of the Ponte Fabrizio,
from *Le antichità romane*, 1756, volume IV plate XVI.
Architectural form as obstruction.

city's spatiality, surrounded by a dense context of residential fabric. In the *vedute*, Piranesi applied the same aesthetic of mass that he saw in the ruins to the buildings of modern Rome. The city appears not as ordered by streets and squares but as an open field punctuated by gigantic and contrasting forms. This urban form renders what Nolli's topography and Vasi's views had downplayed with their urban realism: the geographical and political struggle through which the city had evolved its form. Piranesi renders this form as irreducible to any totalizing order or convention. He seems to suggest that the form of the city is the unsolvable confrontation between the individuality of its parts. The tension of confrontation between forms and their removal from the coherent part-to-whole system of an overall spatial management constitute the paradoxical unity of Piranesi's *instauratio urbis*.

In the map of Rome published at the beginning of the first volume of the *Antichità*, which can be read as a critique of Nolli's Rome, Piranesi removes the modern city, just as he would later propose in the *Campo Marzio*. Significantly, this map is framed by fragments of the *Forma urbis*, an ancient detailed map of Rome engraved in marble and discovered in pieces in 1562, just one year after publication of Ligorio's *Imago urbis*. A fundamental aspect of the *Forma urbis* was its planimetric projection of Rome at a high level of architectural resolution. After working on his own map of Rome, Nolli worked on the fragments of the ancient stone map in order to reconstruct the overall form of ancient Rome, but he gave up on it a few years later due to the overwhelming complexity of the problem. Piranesi probably assisted Nolli in this work, because the title page of the *Antichità romane* with its images of fragments clearly references this unfinished project.[26] These fragments emphasize the impossibility of reconstructing ancient Rome through mere archaeological evidence—that is, through a philological "scientific" method.

Archigymnasio della Sapienza

3.18
Giovanni Battista Piranesi, Archiginnasio
della Sapienza, from *Varie vedute*, 1748.

Palazzo della Cancelleria

Piranesi F

3.19
Giovanni Battista Piranesi, Palazzo della
Cancelleria, from *Varie vedute*, 1748.

Inspired by the scientific methodology of topographic survey, Nolli had approached the reconstruction of ancient Rome as an archaeological problem based on found evidence and devoid of intuitive conjecture or any argumentative thesis other than the need to make the entire topographical form of ancient Rome scientifically legible.

In his incipit to the *Antichità*, Piranesi radically contradicts this approach, suggesting that the restoration of the *true* form of ancient Rome is possible not by relying on mere evidence or by attempting an overall survey of all the topographic layers of the city, but by focusing on the remaining ruins and using them as points of entry for a conjecture about the form of the city. Rather than interpreting the fragments of the *Forma urbis* as evidence to be recomposed in an overall map, he approaches them as partial examples for reinventing Rome. Piranesi treats both the ruins that punctuated the empty field of Rome and the fragments as examples whose forms can only be assumed as analogical and not literal representations of ancient Rome. This approach to ancient Rome made Piranesi's work impossible to categorize as either antiquarian endeavors or projects for a new city.

It is important to stress that Piranesi's knowledge of monuments was supported by careful surveying campaigns. His collaboration with Nolli gave him the most up-to-date knowledge in topographic measurement. His plans, sections, and elevations of monuments appear to be precise and accurate, and he often corrected mistakes of earlier surveys.[27] The pictorial impact of his *vedute* has often overshadowed the impeccable precision with which Piranesi drew plans and elevations of monuments. Yet he systematically altered specific details, such as the real structure of foundations, in a way that makes it impossible to separate the precision and objectivity of his depiction from the invention. In this fusion of precision and invention, Piranesi pursued the analogical knowledge of Rome promoted by the tradition of *in-stauratio urbis*. The *Campo Marzio* was just such an accomplishment of this method.

Il Campo Marzio dell'antica Roma was executed by Piranesi as an attempt to reconstruct the "original" form of imperial Rome in the area of modern Rome. The reconstruction is conjectural, based both on established evidence and on reinvented forms of the ancient city. The survey follows the same method as the *Antichità*, but here Piranesi focuses not on the city but on the part of the city he polemically wants to attack. Like the *Antichità*, the work consisted of a variety of illustrations, from views to topographic reconstructions to depictions of details, all arranged without following a precise trajectory within the city. The most important and well-known part of *Campo Marzio* is the *Ichnographia Campi Martii antiquae urbis*, a topographic reconstruction of the site in which Piranesi drew the plan of every building. The visual effect of the map is unprecedented. In rendering the entire city through the architectural plan of every building, he produced an abundance of information that counters the synthetic approach of scientific surveys of cities. The map is based on the same mix of topographical precision and imagination as his previous work. Some of the complexes were accurately reconstructed by following the existing ruins, but others were drawn according to his imagination. Many artifacts were elaborated following the examples of tombs, which produced the compositional and typological variety characteristic of this map.

Yet the topographic precision with which the map is produced makes the *Campo Marzio* not a romantic or utopian foil to the scientific mapping and survey of cities, but rather a critique of scientific mapping that uses the same instruments and methods of scientific precision. In this sense it is interesting to note the difference between Pirro Ligorio's *Imago* and Piranesi's

Reliquiae substructionum ac rudera theatri Balbi, hodie tumulus in regione, quae dicitur Regulae.
Vide indicem ruinarum num. 81

Tab. XXVIII.

Piranesi F.

3.20
Giovanni Battista Piranesi, "Reliquiae substructionum
ac rudera Theatri Balbi," from *Il Campo Marzio
dell'antica Roma*, 1762, Plate XXVIII.

Ichnographia. Ligorio's reconstruction of Rome was certainly a source of inspiration for Piranesi's antiquarian work, and especially for the *Campo Marzio*. But where the topographic survey of the Campo Marzio was presented as a plan, Ligorio's reconstruction of Rome was based mainly on the images of ancient buildings found on Roman coins. This viewpoint deeply conditioned his approach to architecture, in which the diagram of the elevation overtakes the three-dimensional form of the buildings. As a result, Ligorio's vision of Rome is based more on the visual effects of buildings than on their forms. Piranesi, on the other hand, attempts to go beyond the image of buildings and to understand them through the topographic precision he had learned from Nolli. In this sense, Piranesi did not simply oppose the analogical form of *instauratio urbis* to the topographic precision of scientific survey; in fact, he *returned* to the ideological approach of *instauratio urbis* by incorporating the forms and methods of scientific surveying. Yet, in his hands, scientific survey was no longer an instrument of planning management, but instead a mechanism focused on the polemical invention of architectural form.

This becomes evident when the Nolli map is compared to Piranesi's *Campo Marzio*. Unlike the figure-ground of the Nolli map, Piranesi employed a figure-figure technique in which the city is rendered not as an urban mass punctuated by architectural spaces but as a conjecture of its architectural form. The *Campo Marzio* is a utopian projection of the city devoid of the attributes of urbanity so emphasized by the Nolli maps— the hierarchy of spaces, circulation, and built fabric. Piranesi reinvented Rome as a city without streets. The only means of continuity is the river, whose meandering course is framed by Piranesi as the real protagonist of the plan, diagonally crossing the map from the top right to the bottom left. It is not difficult to imagine what sort of spectacle would be produced when the area flooded—hundreds of monumental complexes would emerge from the water like islands. Piranesi's *Campo Marzio* seems to emerge from such a vision: a city whose potential for possible associations, compositions, and trajectories among its parts is not absorbed by any infrastructural or other overall spatial order.

To fully understand this vision, it is necessary to return to the idea of Rome that emerges in the *Scenographia*, the view of the Campo Marzio that introduces the *Ichnographia*. The *Scenographia* belongs to the tradition of representation of *instauratio urbis*: it shows the city as constituted only by the ruins that had been incorporated in the development of the modern urban form, but with modern Rome removed. The resulting image is neither a mapping nor a restoration of ancient Rome; the *Scenographia* reveals that the premise (and perhaps the goal) of the reconstruction of the ancient form of Rome was the destruction of modern Rome—the destruction of a form that Nolli had represented in all its urban dimensions. Indications of this intention are the astonishing and unique views of the Campo Marzio that Piranesi composed as a compendium to the big map.

While in the *Antichità* Piranesi portrayed the ruins of ancient Rome within their modern context, in the *vedute* for *Campo Marzio* he showed the ruins of what was in his time the most densely populated area of Rome as completely liberated from all other historical layers of the city. Significantly, Piranesi titled these *vedute* "reliquiae substructionum" (relics liberated from subsequent layers of built form), but he did not restore the ruins to their original state. Instead, the ancient complexes appear as forms that are irreducible either to their present condition or to their original state, an aesthetic that Piranesi conjures against the refined forms of baroque Rome and the topographic precision of Nolli.

The result of this operation, which must be seen not only as the heart of the *Campo Marzio* but also as the summa of *instauratio urbis,* was an unprecedented interpretation of the architectural ruin not as something that has succumbed to the course of time, but as something that has survived both time and the modern city. Through Piranesi these ruins are emancipated to become the latent beginning of a new city whose potential is not yet subsumed by any incipient urban order.

As the ruins of Piranesi's *vedute* and *Scenographia* imply, such a beginning is imagined as the selection of the city's constituent elements of autonomous monumental architectures, rather than as an overall plan of the city. The isolation of the ruins reinforces their presence but also creates potential in the spaces between them. Against the managerial logic implied in Nolli's city plan, Piranesi opposed a way of thinking of the city based on conjectures. Here lies the fundamental critique that Piranesi's work implicitly made, not simply of the Nolli map, but of the mentality and values that such a paradigmatic representation of Rome suggested.

The Nolli map illustrates the difference between architecture as finite form and the city as a totality of urban space, which he represented with a diagrammatic blackened mass. This demonstrated that architecture is simply an island within the city, whose urban form far exceeds the possibility of an architectural morphology to accommodate its scale. The conjecture of Piranesi's forms confirms the unbridgeable discrepancy between architectural form and the totality of urban space. This is affirmed in the *Campo Marzio* where the city appears as only buildings, devoid of streets and all the other infrastructural means of continuity that are necessary for a city to function. In this "unplugged" condition of the city, all attributes of urbanity are gone. Rather than interpreting such a scenario as a terminal point of the city, however, Piranesi presents it as a latent beginning embedded within what already exists in urban space—the ruins. The difference between architecture and urban space is radicalized in order to show the architectural clues that allow the critical imagination to rethink the city, not through its managerial practices but as a field of potential possibilities. In this way, Piranesi overcame the insufficiency of architectural form, making it possible to rethink architectural design not as what exhausts the form of the city, but as what opens the potential for imagining it differently.

4 ARCHITECTURE AS A STATE OF EXCEPTION
ÉTIENNE-LOUIS BOULLÉE'S PROJECT FOR A METROPOLIS

In 1967 Aldo Rossi translated into Italian, and wrote an introduction to, Étienne-Louis Boullée's *Architecture, Essay on Art*.[1] Written at the end of the eighteenth century but unpublished until 1953, *Architecture, Essay on Art* can be understood as an architectural treatise in the form of commentary on a series of public monuments that Boullée designed between the last years of the French monarchy and the years immediately after the 1789 Revolution. Some of the buildings Boullée describes were site specific and executed as commissions or competitions, including the Opera Theater (1781) and the Library (1781), while others were theoretical proposals, including the Metropolitan Church (1781), the Justice Palace (1782), and the National Palace (1792), but all of the projects were characterized by the austere composition of simple volumes. Notably, Boullée's *Architecture, Essay on Art* was the first architectural treatise to focus exclusively on public monuments. Boullée's use of the term *monument* is important. Before Boullée, *monument* was used to describe a commemorative building (from *memento*, "remember"). After Boullée, the monument also included any public building housing a public service, such as a theater, library, or museum, and potentially accessible to all.[2] Boullée distinguished the monument from residential architecture, which was defined as "private," or not accessible to all. For this reason he omitted residential architecture, which traditionally constituted the core of architectural treatises, from the essay.[3] Rather than being predicated on celebration or commemoration, Boullée's definition of the monument distinguished public from private; for him, monumental buildings offered no personal or specific element for commemoration. Instead, Boullée's monument addressed and celebrated its use by the anonymous and free individual: the citizen who was governed no longer by a monarchy but by a secular and republican state. Thus a library is a monument to "science," a museum is a temple to "culture." Correspondingly, Boullée's public monuments shared an architectural language based on the composition of anonymous and simple geometrical volumes. These volumes were characterized by two kinds of partitions: bare walls, and densely arranged columns that seem to form walls. The former was Boullée's favorite architectural "ornament" as it produced an architecture made only of shadows, which he considered his most important achievement.[4] The shadows presented nature in its primary perceptual form of light and dark, and Boullée wanted this anonymous, primary, and empirical experience of bare volumes projecting shadows to be the main attribute of the public monument dedicated to the free citizen. Even when he designed a commemorative monument to an individual—the Funeral Cenotaph of Newton, for example—the way he abstracted the subject in the perfect form of a sphere makes clear that it was not so much the person as it was the scientist, or the idea of science, being celebrated by the effect of natural light penetrating the dark interior of the globe.

None of the projects described in the *Essay* was realized, but to see them simply as "visionary" projects overlooks the specific conditions of each proposal, which Boullée articulates in terms of technically inventive and individual approaches to functional, programmatic, and even contextual problems. Indeed, he describes not only what the monuments were intended to symbolize through their "character" or formal references, but also how they responded to specific programmatic and technical requirements such as accessibility, safety, circulation, and, in some cases, site constraints. For example, in his project for the Opera, the extreme geometrical regularity of the form—a cylinder surrounded by columns—not only reinforces its monumental and public nature, but also demonstrates a concern for public welfare with its unprecedented provision for egress in the event of a fire. His theoretical project for a fort departed from the landscape-like form of baroque fortifications and returned to the massive vertical form of the castle. Besides recuperating the monumentality of military architecture, this choice reflected the advances in military architecture introduced by Marc René de Montalembert in his treatise on perpendicular fortifications (in which the eighteenth-century engineer anticipated the form of twentieth-century bunker architecture).[5]

Boullée's work is "exceptional" in its exclusive use of public monuments as a means for a general theory of architecture, and because these monuments respond to specific site and technical conditions. Rossi considered Boullée's manuscript an example of theorizing architecture from within the *poetic* experience of designing specific architectural compositions. He interpreted Boullée's work as a radical manifesto for architectural autonomy intended as the possibility of self-reflection, not on abstract norms but on the making of architecture as exceptional, specific, and finite forms. Understanding Boullée's choice of the monument as a way to emphasize the limits of architecture as a circumscribed, finite object, Rossi was fascinated by the extreme simplicity and austerity with which Boullée represented architecture and the theoretical consistency through which the sequence of these finite forms manifested a design method. He argued that Boullée was the prototypical rationalist architect

4.1
Étienne-Louis Boullée, project for an Opera House,
1781. (Bibliothèque Nationale de Paris.)

because he had established a few "logical principles" through which it was possible to address any design problem; according to Rossi, these principles were the idea of composition achieved through the paratactic juxtaposition of simple geometrical forms; the use of natural effects such as the play of light and shadow; and the distributive clarity of a building—the primary attribute of a public monument. Even though these logical principles sought to establish an intelligible, and thus transmissible, architecture, Rossi noted that Boullée had not applied them as a totalizing system of norms; that approach would later typify the work of Boullée's most important student, Jean-Nicolas-Louis Durand. Instead, Boullée illustrated these principles through the design of exceptional finite forms. Rossi thus seems to suggest that *Architecture, Essay on Art* was based on the invention of a few exemplary architectural compositions which, by repeating certain principles, even within the finite scheme of a series of monuments, had the potential to define a general approach to architecture.

Although Boullée explicitly described the sequence of monuments in the *Essay* as a "project for a metropolis," Rossi concludes that Boullée's text has no connection to the city. Having just published *The Architecture of the City*,[6] Rossi seems to have needed to focus on a text in which, as he wrote, architecture was analyzed *in vacuo*, as a pure act of architectural autonomy apart from the problems of the city. Unlike his thinking in *The Architecture of the City*, Rossi's introduction to the *Essay* focuses not on the structural relationship between the typological datum of the city and the urban artifact, but on the artifact itself as a composition devoid of any external constraint other than the architect's self-imposed logical principles. I propose to counter Rossi's interpretation, not by denying his argument, but by demonstrating how Boullée's logical principles produced an "autonomous" architecture that can be read as an attempt to condense and represent in the monument the formal attributes that characterized the urban development of Paris in the seventeenth and eighteenth centuries.

Historians have emphasized that the evolution of Paris in this period can be seen as paradigmatic of the formation of the formal, social, and political spatiality of the modern metropolis. In the spatiality produced by the extension of cities toward a territorial, or regional, organization, architecture became more and more reified in the diffusion of generic residential types and the management of circulation. Boullée's monuments, reduced to anonymous, almost abstract bare volumes in which circulation plays a large role, go beyond simply displaying and radicalizing the spatial attributes of the emerging modern metropolis: by translating these spatial attributes into finite forms, they also suggest an implicit critical project. This critical project rendered in a series of intelligible finite forms the effects of the ubiquitous forces that shaped the emergence of modern metropolitan space. Boullée's principles were a reflection of architecture not only as an autonomous discipline but also as a project on the city, and his theory both exhibits and counters the spatial transformations of the city. In other words, the scale and composition of his architecture manifest a new vision of the public, as exemplified through his civic monuments, and provide a limit to the totalizing spatiality implied in the evolving tradition of so-called French classicism and its urban applications. In this context, Boullée's project was not a "revolutionary" negation of the existing architectural tradition, but rather a critical, postrevolutionary appropriation of this tradition for addressing public space.

Boullée's project for the metropolis, which is implied in his theory of architecture, is grounded in the discourse of subjects, institutions, and architectural forms that marked the development

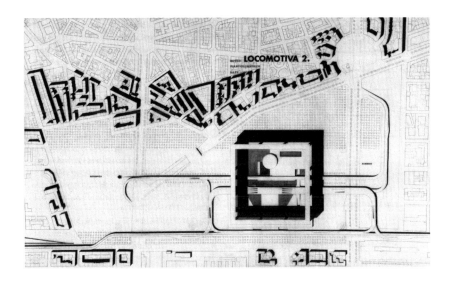

4.2
Aldo Rossi, Luca Meda, and Gianugo Polesello,
competition entry for the Business District in Turin,
1962. Competition entry.

of Paris during the seventeenth and eighteenth centuries. In my reading of this architectural development, I intend to go beyond the stylistic terms, such as baroque, rococo, and neoclassicism, through which the history of French architecture has traditionally been defined. At stake in this development and in the conceptual and formal foundations of Boullée's project was the establishment of a new form of publicness that evoked vastness and uniformity as attributes of urban space. With the emergence of the *hôtel* and the square, this new spatiality was inserted into the existing fabric of Paris; it also formed a very urban infrastructure through the opening of boulevards and the engineering of city space, which became a paradigm of modern *metropolitan* space.

Beginning in the early sixteenth century, the ancient idea of the *nation* was reformulated within a new political concept of the *state*. Over some two hundred years, until the mid 1700s, the nation-state evolved by centralizing sovereignty and undermining regimes such as feudalism and the Catholic Church. In the seventeenth century, this political paradigm, of which France was the most important manifestation, not only consolidated power toward an *absolutist* monarchy as the form of the state, but also reacted to the problem of religious conflict that had plagued Europe since the Reformation. One of the political consequences of the establishment of the nation-state as a paradigm of sovereignty was the beginning of a progressive secularization of society. This process began with relative religious tolerance and increasingly relied on initiatives to secularize social relationships, such as Henri IV's elevation of the *noblesse de robe*, an aristocracy linked to the growing power of the state's bureaucracy. The new prerogatives of the *noblesse de robe* in the administration of justice, bureaucracy, and public finance gave rise to a truly metropolitan aristocracy. The lifestyle, attitudes, and cultural pursuits of this class can be seen as a fundamental cultural and social origin of the bourgeoisie's political rise in the late eighteenth and early nineteenth centuries. Though the *noblesse de robe* was still a "court society" bound to the hierarchical forms of the *ancien régime* city, the rising bourgeoisie would be linked to the increasing social and economic mobility of the modern metropolis, brought about by the rise of scientific thought at the turn of the nineteenth century. And yet the metropolitan anonymity of the bourgeois city is unthinkable without the normative and bureaucratic abstraction that originated with the introduction of the *noblesse de robe* and that constituted the political essence of what is called French classicism.[7]

Architecturally, French classicism represents the rise of a systemic architecture and urban design that developed in parallel with the consolidation of the nation-state's sovereignty and the emergence of the *noblesse de robe* as the new ruling class. Unlike in Italy, where classicism arose during the Renaissance, between the fifteenth and sixteenth centuries, in France it developed during the baroque period in the seventeenth century. Where the Italian baroque was synonymous with a growing formal complexity, French classicism was a style of public representation based on the diffusion of canons and formal simplification. Italian classicism had produced influential architecture and treatises, but due to unending political instability in Italy, it had a limited impact on the reformation of the city, the medieval character of which remained until the nineteenth century. The political stability that characterized France in the seventeenth century made it possible to implement and further develop the classicist canons that in Italy were limited to exceptional structures such as palazzi, churches, and monumental squares. In politics, as in architecture and urbanism, French classicism designated an approach more inclined toward norms than exceptions, toward regularity rather than complexity. In architecture, the systematic approach of French classicism was manifested in well-organized and diffused pedagogy, such as the seminal theoretical work of François Blondel. Blondel's influential *Cours d'architecture*, which was published beginning in 1675 and remained an important text for over a century, is an example of the systematic diffusion of architecture as an *esprit de système* based on strict rules and proportions.[8] The same way of thinking is found in the theories of Claude Perrault. In a treatise on the five classical orders published in 1683, Perrault polemically attacked Blondel's rigid system of proportions and argued for a mathematical ordering of the classical rule, which would rationalize and simplify the use of the orders according to the mathematical relationships of their different proportions. Ultimately Perrault suggested an average proportion based on the best architectural examples in order to produce a single cohesive system. The effectiveness of these teachings, both in the making of architecture and in the ordering of a more systemic and scientific approach to architecture, narrowed the gap between theory and practice in France and aided the circulation of an "average" and "normative" classical language within the city itself.

A fundamental "political" contribution to the diffusion of this classical language was the creation in 1671 of the Académie Royale d'Architecture by Louis XIV's minister of finance, Jean-Baptiste Colbert, as the outgrowth of his Conseil des Bâtiments, of which Blondel was the first director.[9] The institutional emancipation of *architecture* from *building* further separated architectural language from the mere "art of building" and invested that language with a means of diffuse political power. At the same time, Colbert conveyed systems for architecture by means of lectures, courses, and ateliers, and disseminated these teachings through texts. With the Académie, Colbert created a radically new way to organize architecture that explained it not only as a technical or artistic competence but also as a veritable form of *organizational* knowledge that could be developed and transmitted systematically. In this way, purveyors of architectural knowledge aimed to establish a formal and political consensus by defining the examples of a new state-based architecture. These examples, such as public buildings initiated through competitions among architects or prizes awarded to projects executed by promising young students of architecture, would help to spread state-controlled architecture in both the city and the nation. The fundamental strength of Colbert's Académie was that this diffusion operated not by imposing a particular architectural style, but rather by promoting clarity as the fundamental quality of a public architectural knowledge. This emphasis on clarity often coincided with the development of a systematic architectural language, which resulted in an architecture characterized by austerity and a combinatory logic that would have a great influence on French architects, gradually liberating them from the proportional and ornamental logic of the classical orders. This evolution of architectural pedagogy based on attributes such as clarity, austerity, and the combinatory logic of form would serve as the foundation of Boullée's simple forms. Yet Boullée's monuments would transform these attributes from their normative control of the city into an archipelago of finite formal and spatial "states of exception."

To understand Boullée, it is first necessary to reconsider how the establishment of the systematic simplification and standardization of architectural language took its cue from the architecture of the city of Paris and the development of exemplary urban forms. The three most powerful forms of architecture and urbanity that were inspired by the systematic language of French classicism were the courtyard, the square, and the axis. These took the respective forms of the *hôtel*, *place*, and *boulevard*.

The *hôtel* can be seen as the originating type of a spatiality that emerged within the city of French classicism. As an urban version of the *château*, the *hôtel* first appeared in the sixteenth century, and its development in Paris at the beginning of the seventeenth century is closely linked to the emergence of the *noblesse de robe*.[10] Embodying a typology of the palace adopted by the new urban aristocracy, the *hôtel* was radically different from the archetype of the Italian Renaissance palazzo. Where the palazzo was defined as a self-sufficient block with an interior courtyard, presenting the city with a closed exterior facade, the *hôtel* conflated the main facade with the courtyard to create a singular concave entity with a defining entrance. The typical formal definition of the *hôtel* was a response to the difficulty of inserting regular spaces into the fabric of the city. Like any other medieval city, Paris in the sixteenth and seventeenth centuries had a very irregular topography. In order to create the symmetry and regularity of the aristocratic residence, a regular space—the courtyard—had to be placed at the center of the site, which was open on one side to the street. The courtyard was closed off from the street by a simple wall or by a one-story building, and the elements of the residence were organized as a U-shaped building around the courtyard. In contrast with the complex fabric of the city, the *hôtel* defined a regular "hollow" space that enabled the regular pattern of the *hôtel* facades. The courtyard spaces framed by the *hôtels* became the model of a new urban spatiality made of regular forms, in clear opposition to the irregular spatiality of the medieval city.

This regular spatiality also characterized another important urban space that began to emerge in Paris in the seventeenth century: the *place*, or square. The *place* is based on the same formal principle as the *hôtel*: a void carved into the intricate fabric of the city to create a space. Instead of belonging to a single owner as the *hôtel* did, the *place* had a collective of different owners. In this organization, houses that faced the *place* shared the same facade, which framed an architectural space much like an enlarged *hôtel*

4.3
François Mansart, Hôtel de la Villière, 1635. Carving
a regular space within the intricacy of the city.

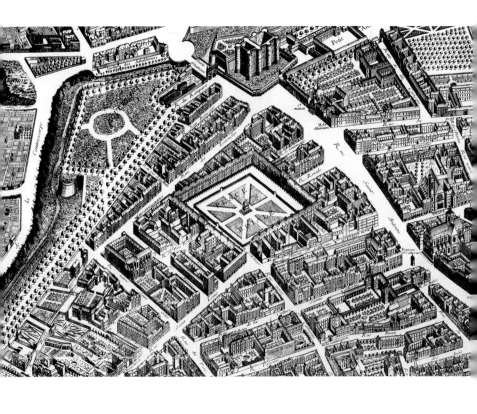

4.4
Place Royale, bird's-eye view. Monumental
architecture as void.

courtyard. Uniform fenestration and predominant horizontal lines strongly united the four sides of the facades bounding it, making the *place* the fulcrum of a rational reform of the city structure. The most paradigmatic example is the Place Royale, built by Henri IV.[11] The Place Royale embodied an important, radically new conception of urban space and its relationship to power. Its aggregation of surrounding buildings into one urban system can be seen as an early form of optimizing urban development, which would mature in a series of uniform and monumental squares and, later, in the bourgeois boulevards that Baron Georges-Eugène Haussmann established after the Revolution of 1848. In these uniform spaces, power was manifested as a spatial whole, an "urban room," and a form that brought together different elements in one universally applicable typology of public space. The squares built in the seventeenth and eighteenth centuries in Paris, such as the Place Royale and Louis XIV's Place Vendôme and Place des Victoires, both designed by Jules Hardouin-Mansart, gave built form a political power that was total and ubiquitous. Importantly, rather than being represented by a monumental building, this political power was presented through a uniform architectural framework that, because of its regularity, could be repeated throughout the entire city.

It is in this context that one should consider the radical anonymity of the so-called *architecture d'accompagnement* that corresponded to the emergence and rise of a bourgeois middle class in the seventeenth and eighteenth centuries. This architecture, made of a simple row of windows and false arcades, was inspired by the spatiality of the *hôtels*, squares, and uniform streets, and later defined the generic character of the nineteenth-century bourgeois city. Pierre Le Muet's *Manière de bastir pour touttes sortes de personnes* (1623) can be considered the theoretical source of this emerging middle-class "generic city."[12] Le Muet referred to "every type of person" as if the architectural attributes of classical décor would now address all social classes. According to Le Muet's principles, symmetry drives a system of architectural composition designed to produce a normative, anonymous aesthetic. The schematic and simplified facades he proposed implied that a single order could organize an entire block, an entire street, and an entire city.

This line of development was finally summarized in Pierre Patte's famous *Partie du plan général de Paris* (1765), a map of Paris in which the city is defined by a series of urban spaces based on the entries to a competition to design a new royal square. By including all of the competition entries in one plan, Patte generalized this prototype as a possible project for the entire center of Paris.[13] This plan can be interpreted as both a project and a mapping: a recognition and composition of the trend in defining the city by means of monumental empty spaces such as the Place Royale, Place Vendôme, and Place des Victoires. It is interesting to note how the map is drawn. The squares and the streets linking them are highlighted in the city fabric itself by reinforcing the line of the facades framing them. Viewed as a paradigmatic representation of the city, this map radically changed the figure-ground relationship that had traditionally linked monuments to the city. In Patte's plan, the figure of the monument as an isolated object has been replaced by its negative in the form of a concave space.

By presenting the logic of the concave space of the square as the dominant urban form, Patte also expands the logic of the *hôtel*'s extroverted courtyard into a system for the city itself, resulting in an archipelago of squares. Patte's plan reduces architecture to mere background, so that circulation—the efficient movement of people and commodities through the city—becomes not only the form but also the spectacle of the city itself. Circulation was finally acknowledged as the new imperative of the city. Without creating a master plan for the entire city, Patte reinvented the

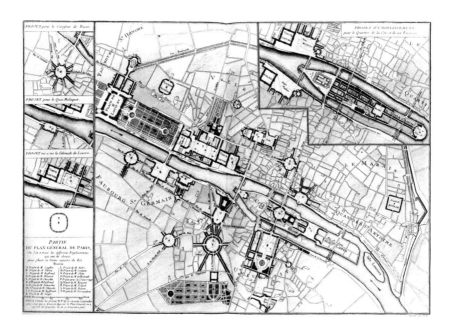

4.5
Pierre Patte, *Partie du plan général de Paris*, 1765.
Patte produced this urban plan in conjunction with the
competition for designs for Place Louis XV. The city is
composed of an archipelago of voids of circulation and
space, the main themes of the emerging metropolis.

city using a rational language that reduced the problem of urban space to one of delineating voids. Though he could not define the city's circulation with the technical competence and precision of the engineers who were then emerging as more effective practitioners in shaping the city, the architecture of the city implied by his plan proposed a scenario that anticipated the metropolitan scale of nineteenth-century Paris.

Boullée's public monuments are conceptually related to Patte's plan in their scale and design. The very form of Boullée's monuments, with their strong symmetry, their autonomy, and their dislocation in the city, can be seen as conceptually "molded" by Patte's archipelago of squares. In fact, Boullée's isolated monuments can be read as a "positive" developed as a response to the "negative" of Patte's squares. As a summary of the urban transformations of Paris, Patte's plan not only literally indicated the *place* as the new scale of urban development, but also announced the scale and architecture of another urban element that would further expand the unifying logic of the *hôtel* and the *place*: this was the boulevard.

With Louis XIV's demolition of the city walls in 1670, the form of the city finally broke its ancient constraints. The *bollwerk*—the expansive system of fortifications that used to enclose cities within geometrically complex earthworks—became the *boulevard*, a broad system of circulation that acquired its scale precisely by incorporating the new "extra-city" space created by the removal of the city walls. Significantly, what had once limited and enclosed the city was now transformed into a system that expanded the city's circulation and, by implication, produced the possibility of endless growth. The demolition of the fortifications was the most clear and aggressive manifestation of the way economic transactions and urban development were linked, ready to become the very form of the new urban expansion. With the removal of its walls, the city could no longer be conceived as an autonomous entity placed within a territory from which it had been disconnected by its defensive system. The new metropolis now became the hub of the nation-state, where concentration and decentralization were simultaneously organized as part of the process of the circulation and distribution of people, resources, and commodities.

Circulation thus became the sine qua non of these emerging cities. The invention of the boulevard can be seen as the urban form that blurred the distinction between the city and the territory around it, conflating it into one system. As enormous structures, these boulevards were isolated from the city fabric, confronted with a seemingly endless amount of residential space organized by the new axes of mobility. The planting of trees on both sides of the boulevard added to its uniformity, giving the boulevard a visually identifiable border.

Within this generic grammar of the city based on pattern, repetition, and the insistence on the horizontal over the vertical, one finally approaches the architectural dimension that Boullée critically sublimated in his architectural language of large and simple forms placed in vast open landscapes. Before addressing Boullée's architecture, it is useful to analyze the way the emerging grammar of the city unfolded in a new regional and generic dimension, where architecture as form disappeared: the engineering of the region.

Whereas the architect addressed the new paradigm of the city as a space of circulation, the engineer designed plans and policies for the management of the larger region in order to exploit its full productivity. For the engineer, nature was synonymous with production. Thus, unlike the architect, the eighteenth-century French civil engineer did not work within an established canon of rules, but rather continuously rationalized his method of design according to the empirical needs of land management and the emergent potential of natural resources. For this reason, the engineering of the territory is closely linked to the mastery of technological progress. As Antoine Picon has argued, the work of engineers in France in the eighteenth and nineteenth centuries was not simply a form of competence but a paradigmatic attitude toward the city.[14] Michel Foucault describes this paradigm in his studies of the emergence of territorial governance.[15] In territorial governance, Foucault writes, the dynamic of exchange prevailed over the singularity of places, and the improvement of infrastructure and mobility became engineering's most urgent concern. Rather than being an open-ended form of progress, however, the development of infrastructure was closely linked to the need to optimize the productivity of the land, the mobility of workers, and the exchange of commodities. With this logic, the equilibrium of supply and demand was seen as a new form of natural equilibrium. The economic pressure to control the region led to the attempt to scientifically map its features; such mapping produced a new definition of space as a complex of transactions, movement, and services that extended beyond the boundaries of localities. The geography of a region was thus reorganized by these maps in terms of economic control and exploitation, which led to the emergence of engineering as an extremely sophisticated form of state control, beyond the traditional form of military force. Indeed, this new institutional control was wielded not through war and conquest but through colonization by infrastructural "improvements." In this way the traditional use of violent imposition and enmity—the bases of political institutions—was transformed and concealed by the economic criteria of "utility." The idea of utility allowed the concept of reason to be subsumed within the control of economic calculation and accumulation. Civil engineering became a tactic of spatial organization that blended similarities and differences, norms and exceptions, in one total and flexible system of knowledge. The increasing relevance of the École Polytechnique and Durand's architectural response to it with his gridded, and thus normative, approach to design are examples of this system. While architecture as an object was seen as less relevant, the engineers absorbed the idea of architecture as a form of the organization of space. Engineering did not reject the epistemic premises of the architectural treatise with its will to a systematic organization of knowledge, but expanded that systematic logic from the physical embodiment of space to its management. In this expansion, the criteria of the orders and the combination of geometric forms into one coherent whole were replaced by the ideal of utility as the new social and political whole. At the core of utility was precisely what the urban development of Paris was forecasting: unimpeded circulation, the economic utopia of laissez-faire politics.

The hierarchical and combinatory nature of the architectural treatise, with its norms, orders, and classifications, was thus translated into the managerial practice of the engineering of the territory, seen as a site of production. As Picon writes, "Whereas architects had argued for a form of production which was regulated by a freely agreed adherence to the same formal language, which they tried to render ever more transparent, the engineers proposed a compactness of entities, which they had first of all sought to unify, and then the abrupt revelation of the tension thus created."[16] For this reason, engineering initially was applied not to the city but to the countryside of the territory. As a complex of resources—agricultural fields, timber forests, and mines—the countryside was considered to be the productive realm, while the old dense city with its problems of congestion and conflict was seen as increasingly unproductive, and thus in need of reorganization as a regional form.

Thus, the modern city can be seen as the translation of the idea of productive landscape into the space of the city. Through its managerial practices, which fuse public and private within the idea of utility, engineering transformed the city into an endlessly expanding landscape in constant flux and with continual exchange. Supported by the development of science and technology, the new regional city had no form that was not determined by the constantly shifting forces of circulation. For example, the theories of the city advanced by Marc-Antoine Laugier, who compared the design of the city to a forest, and Claude-Nicolas Ledoux, whose proto-industrial plan for Chaux was influenced by the Physiocratic theories of economic management, both reflect the new paradigm of utility and management as the basis of the emerging eighteenth-century metropolis.[17] It is precisely within this context of a new spatiality, born from the tradition and typologies of French classicist architecture and evolved through the urban transformation of the landscape as a site of production, that architects increasingly diminished the role of the classical orders and decoration in favor of the "free," and thus more flexible, composition of volumes in the landscape. This "autonomy of form"—which Emil Kaufmann describes as the main attribute of the work of the "revolutionary architects" of the late eighteenth century[18]—manifested architects' awareness of the new constraints imposed by the emerging spatiality of production. Boullée's formal vocabulary must be seen in this context. Here the composition of volumes in a landscape is not simply assumed and theorized as a necessity, but is emphasized as holding the possibility for architecture to emancipate itself from mere utility and to become a form of critical judgment. As he declared, "Nothing is beautiful if all is not judicious."[19] This understanding of rationality in terms of judgment, rather than as mere utility, made Boullée's architecture highly critical of its

own context in the emerging productive metropolis. For Boullée, the manifestation of judgment in architecture is the act of
composition.

The composition of simple volumetric forms—not the proportions of the orders or the engineer's management of the city—is
the central theme of Boullée's theory of architecture. Yet it is possible to argue that Boullée's will to composition manifests itself
in the way that the sequence of public monuments is framed, not
as a list of buildings, but, as he declares near the end of *Architecture, Essay on Art*, as exemplary public monuments for a metropolis. If we understand Boullée's sequence of monumental public
buildings as a "project for a metropolis," this project can be seen
as an archipelago of architectural states of exception that counter
a metropolitan space dominated by the extensive management of
production. Against the dynamic fluidity of management, Boullée presents architecture at its degree zero of form: a composition
of elementary and self-limiting volumes.

In their elementary form, projects such as the church of the
Madeleine and the extension of Versailles had already shifted
the emphasis from decoration and proportion to an architecture made of the paratactic juxtaposition of simple geometrical
volumes. This is the case in Boullée's reelaboration of his project for the Madeleine as a "Metropolitan Church." He designed
this building as the composition of a vast cruciform volume,
a cylinder, and a hemisphere, all juxtaposed without any solution of continuity. The interior is a vast space framed by walls
of columns supporting a gigantic vault made of a dense pattern of
panels. The same motif of columns as a wall of densely patterned
vertical lines appears on the exterior. This insistent repetition
of only a few motifs throughout a building is a constant in Boullée's work. He translated the uniformity and equality of bare walls
into a variety of patterns: walls made by columns (Metropolitan

Church), by books (Library), by texts (National Palace), cannonballs (Fortress), arches (Coliseum), doors (Opera). In each case Boullée endlessly repeated a single element, so that even an opening like a door, or a single element like a column, became part of a uniform pattern. Sometimes these elements referred to the program of the building in a familiar, almost naïve way, like the books for the library or the cannonballs for the fortress, but their repetition estranged their familiarity in the same way that a rapidly repeated word slowly loses its familiar sound and becomes something other. This compositional technique can be seen in Boullée's projects for the Metropolitan Church and the Museum, where, as in a Greek temple, the span between the columns is reduced to a minimum so that their sequence appears to be a horizontal screen of densely patterned vertical lines. These patterns seem to exaggerate the repetition of the forms of the emerging metropolis. In this sense, both the patterns and the bare walls of Boullée's architecture can be understood as an analogy of the process of architectural abstraction implied in French classicism, but now developed to its logical end. It is possible to see the walls of Boullée's finite objects as mirroring and emphasizing the uniformity of the architecture of squares and the boulevards framed by "walls" made of endless rows of trees.

For this reason, Boullée's simple geometrical volumes, juxtaposed and presented in the open landscape, reveal not just the flexible, combinatory logic of architectural form in the absence of the static classical orders, but also the purity of simple geometrical volumes, their irreducible autonomy, and the act of composition as the will to put together irreducibly different elements without blurring the juncture that separates them. In this way, composition is exalted both by what is put together and by how that arrangement emphasizes the separation of its parts, thus evoking a sense of stoppage within the continuity of space.

In Boullée's radical embrace of composition, this "separation" becomes the ultimate index of the separateness of all things, and thus of the possibility to make a decision, in the original sense of "to cut" (*decaedere*). Boullée's use of bare walls adorned only by the play of light and shadow is, on the one hand, the evocation of the endless and anonymous architecture and spaces of the emerging metropolis, and on the other, the analogy of a barrier—an *obstruction*—to the flux that shapes such a metropolis.

But, since Boullée's projects are often represented *in vacuo*, or in what appear to be natural or empty landscapes, where is that metropolis? In fact, this method is an analogical representation of the metropolis that illustrates the impossibility of "architecturally" representing—and thus making—the metropolis as a limitless territory of flows. In his stubborn focus on the architectural object isolated in its context, Boullée seems to suggest a strategic retreat of architecture from the city and into "architecture": a circumscribed form that encloses the space of a finite place.

When Boullée was working in Paris, before the Revolution, the metropolis was envisioned as a sequence of singular spaces. After the Revolution, the metropolis had become a vast complex of movement and transactions that exceeded any finite place. At best, the metropolis could be represented as an open landscape, an extensive scene. This was precisely the setting of Boullée's metropolitan buildings. Given such a landscape, the anonymous simplicity of his architecture and its grammar of generic and infinitely repeated elements gave up any architectural pretension to decoration and formal complexities in order to concentrate instead on what architecture could still control: its finite form, its monumental objecthood.

For Boullée, architecture was the opposite of engineering's emergent managerial practice, because architecture could be conceived as a system of static objects rather than one of circulatory

4.6
Étienne-Louis Boullée, design for a Metropolitan
Church, exterior view, 1781–1782. (Bibliothèque
Nationale de Paris.)

flows. Yet it is a mistake to think of Boullée's architecture of finite forms as a romantic gesture of resistance opposed to the forces of the metropolis. While his bare walls may appear in elevation as obstructions, in plan they frame and organize circulation in public monuments. This idea of publicness, which Boullée emphasized as the precondition for architecture that triggers access, would become the primary compositional theme of his plans. This is evident in his projects for public institutions, such as the Museum, the National Palace, and the Municipal Palace. In the plans of these projects, the parts are organized in order to efficiently frame spaces that allow for the free access and circulation of great numbers of people. In this respect, Boullée also seems to exaggerate the logic of urban spaces developed within the tradition of French classicism, such as the *hôtel* courtyard.

An impressive example of Boullée's appropriation of these urban spaces is his project for the National Library. As is well known, the library was to be located in the *hôtel* of Cardinal Mazarin, which Boullée was to adapt to accommodate a large collection of books and a spacious reading room. The structure of the *hôtel* posed a problem because the long and narrow wings framing the courtyard were difficult spaces for managing a library's control and distribution. Moreover, storing the books in these wings was extremely risky, for a fire in the adjacent buildings could easily spread here. Boullée's solution, made in one gesture, was to cover the existing *hôtel* courtyard, transforming it into one gigantic indoor room. In this room, he echoed the uniform pattern of the *hôtel* courtyard by excessively repeating two elements: recessed panels in the vaulted ceiling, and rows of books that served as the framing walls of the room. The inspiration for this solution, Boullée wrote, came from Raphael's fresco *The School of Athens*, which had in turn been inspired by Bramante's project for St. Peter's basilica. In spite of this appropriation, which may have been an a posteriori reference, Boullée's solution seems to elaborate the compositional principles of the urban architecture of Paris, with its particular emphasis on the city's uniform patterns and horizontal lines, to develop the space of an enclosed form that is also an interior public space. In vaulting a courtyard—the space between the wings—Boullée seems to anticipate the vast halls of such public facilities as train stations, in which the scale of the enclosed space reaches the limit of architectural space to contain circulation and void. Circulation plays a fundamental role also in Boullée's project for the Monument to the Supreme Being. Reminiscent of the temple of Fortuna Primigenia in Palestrina (a ruin that was also the inspiration for Bramante's Belvedere and Palladio's Villa Rotonda), the monument is at the top of a vast volumetric composition of terraces and stairs that frames the base of a mountain, which serves as the protagonist of the whole composition. In this sequence of terraces, the diagonal movement of the connecting ramps is the only break from the strong horizontality of the composition. Boullée adopted a similar strategy for his Museum project, in which an enormous ramp, covered by an immense barrel vault, is the only "active" element. In this composition, hierarchies and images disappear within an architecture made purely of light and shadow. At a time when the real protagonist of the vast and rapidly expanding territory was the directionless movement of people, Boullée's projects could be seen as "miniatures" of the vast spaces of the emerging metropolis. Through analogies such as Edmund Burke's concept of the sublime, Boullée's constructed effects exemplified the way the city is made of anonymous forms and their (infinite) repetition.

The best example of Boullée's conception of architecture in terms of its public access and circulation is his project for a Coliseum. After the Revolution, Boullée proposed the Coliseum as a place for public festivals at which an enormous mass of citizens

4.7
Étienne-Louis Boullée, design for a Library, view of
the interior of the second version, 1785. (Bibliothèque
Nationale de Paris.)

could celebrate the "national well-being." Because his major concern was the safety of this large structure, the main form of the monument is its accessibility. For Boullée, any other aspect was redundant, because what matters architecturally in a coliseum is the movement of masses of citizens and the spectacle of these masses seated in the tribunes. As he writes in the *Essay*, "Imagine three hundred thousand people gathered in an amphitheatre where none could escape the eyes of the crowd. The effect produced by this combination of circumstances would be unique. The spectators would be the elements of this surprising spectacle and they alone would be responsible for its beauty."[20] Methods of circulation compose the rest of the structure: "countless" staircases that take spectators to the tribune, and galleries that would protect the crowd from the rain.

In its absolute formal symmetry and sameness, the Coliseum sublimated its urban context. Indeed, Boullée strategically placed this gathering and exhibition of a crowd within the heart of the emerging territorial metropolis: the Étoile at the top of the Champs-Élysées. In this place of constant movement, Boullée's Coliseum analogically sublimated flows and circulation in the concrete limits of a form that constituted a machine for gathering a crowd. Together with the bare walls, the assembling and staging of the crowd is thus the analogical figure par excellence in Boullée's metropolis, achieved through two fundamental architectural principles: symmetry and the sameness of formal elements.

While symmetry, with its perfect correspondence of the parts to the whole, constituted a long tradition in architectural treatises, in Boullée's architecture, symmetry is treated also (and especially) as a logical consequence of equality expressed through the sameness of forms. The users of his buildings are masses of anonymous citizens. Symmetry is used as a compositional logic that guarantees the building's maximum legibility, and thus its public accessibility. Thus Boullée's architecture staged equality not so much in terms of social and symbolic representation but in terms of a formal perception. His vast, uniform, symmetrical, and thus equal spaces destabilized the hierarchies that architecture always exhibited. Instead of following the principles of symmetry and uniformity that characterized the tradition of French classicism as a norm, Boullée developed them as "states of exception" in the form of singular monuments that strategically punctuated and thus opposed the endlessness of the emerging metropolis.

For this reason Boullée's architectural projects, like Palladio's villas, can be seen as analogous cities that, through their finite exemplary objects, stage and define the features of an emerging urban paradigm: the modern metropolis. Because the modern metropolis and its flows are unrepresentable, architecture can only be a frame; but in the act of containment, that frame made of bare walls *reveals* movement. Far from being self-referential, Boullée's bare walls are an analogy of the process of architectural abstraction implied in French classicism, and now developed to its ultimate end. Once the forms of the emerging metropolis born out of the *esprit de système* of French classicism were liberated from the power that had made them effective, the abstraction of the bare walls would celebrate equality not as a social effect but as a political attribute.

If the spaces of the emerging metropolis were molded by an emphasis on circulation and exchange, Boullée's large but ultimately finite spaces retain the "hollowness" of the new metropolitan spaces as the product of a compositional act. This act is one of judgment regarding the forces that produced these spaces. As Rossi writes, Boullée's architecture is not just the form of "rationalism" *sic et simpliciter*, but the form of an "exalted rationalism"— a rationalism that was not in the spirit of a calculus but one of

4.8
Étienne-Louis Boullée, design for a Coliseum, second
version, section view, 1782. (Bibliothèque Nationale
de Paris.)

subjective instrumentality—and thus provides the possibility of judging and taking a position on the city and its institutions.[21] In this context, Boullée's architectural visions can be understood as an attempt to produce, at the very heart of a new and vastly extended metropolis, an exemplary formal and political subjectivity. Contrary to the generic revolutionary attitude often wrongly attributed to Boullée, this subjectivity echoed the very core of the French Revolution's political form: Jacobinism. Beyond simply evoking the liberal freedom of the bourgeois class, these clearly defined volumetric compositions standing within the endlessness of space in the metropolis also evoke the autonomy of the political will, free from the social and economic constraints of a society that was at the heart of the politics of the French Revolution. Boullée renders the republican ideals of the French Revolution not through iconography, but through his emphasis on composition as the core of any architectural decision.

Rossi's interest in Boullée's *Architecture, Essay on Art* showed his preference for an architecture generated by using a few logical principles to produce a composition of simple geometrical forms. Yet for Rossi, Boullée's preference for simplicity was not motivated by the necessity to make architecture conform to the dry mechanism of rules. Instead, Rossi seems to suggest that within Boullée's theoretical work there coexists the need for a method and a radically subjective approach, which results in a theory of architecture composed only of Boullée's own projects. For this reason, Rossi distinguishes between Boullée's "razionalismo esaltato" (exalted rationalism) and the rationalism of French classicism, which he defines as "razionalismo convenzionale" (conventional rationalism). Rossi identifies the latter in the legacy of most architectural treatises and manuals, and in the normative research of the functionalist architects of the twentieth century. For Rossi, conventional rationalism is a normative apparatus composed of descriptions of the classical orders, techniques of construction, and programmatic taxonomies that preceded the making of architecture and from which architecture was supposed to derive its forms. On the other hand, he defines exalted rationalism as a method in which the subjective decision to produce a certain architectural composition leads to the definition of the logical principles necessary for the transmission of that architectural composition. While conventional rationalism predicates an architecture in which norms automatically produce their application, exalted rationalism postulates an architecture in which the decisions regarding a specific architectural form are exceptional moments that define the framework for principles.

Rossi's distinction between the approaches to architecture defined by conventional rationalism and exalted rationalism, and his appraisal of the latter in the work of Boullée, is similar to Carl Schmitt's theory of the state of exception.[22] According to Schmitt, it is not the norm that eventually produces the exception; it is the exception that produces the *order* necessary to be able to conceive and apply norms. Schmitt wanted to emphasize the priority of the subjective decision to apply certain norms over the mere application of norms. He argues that subjective decisions are not "arbitrary" but rather manifest the way the acting subject positions itself toward the essential problems and dilemmas of life. If a normative approach pretends to subsume essential problems and dilemmas within a totalizing apparatus in which the application of a norm is prescribed by another norm, then the theory of the state of exception addresses the priority of decisions and their exceptional and conjunctural form in establishing a framework in which norms are thus applicable.

Unlike the tradition of architectural treatises and manuals and the normative approach to the city that evolved within traditional French classicism, Boullée's exalted rationalism reinvented the legacy of that tradition as a subjective creative act. In other words, Boullée did not negate the effects of the tradition of French classicism on the architecture of the city of Paris; his work even recuperated French classicism's most salient traits, such as uniformity, the prevalence of horizontal lines, the concave spatiality of *hôtel* courtyards and royal squares, and the vast space of the emerging metropolitan city. But he developed these effects through the exceptional terms of subjective compositions that resulted in finite form-objects. Whereas the making of modern spatiality, as exemplified by the transformation of Paris during the seventeenth and eighteenth centuries, evolved toward the totalizing space of circulation—in which architecture was more and more dissolved within the infinite space of urbanization—Boullée critiqued this tendency with the enclosed space and finite form of his public monuments. And the architecture of these monuments was made by recapitulating, in exceptional terms, the forms and experiences of an urban tendency, not as a ubiquitous force but as a finite, and thus critical, form.

5 THE CITY WITHIN THE CITY
OSWALD MATHIAS UNGERS, OMA,
AND THE PROJECT OF THE CITY AS ARCHIPELAGO

In the 1970s, West Berlin faced an ongoing urban crisis. Following the destruction of the Second World War, the division of Germany into two opposing blocks, and the partition of Berlin into two cities—East Berlin as the capital of the Democratic Republic of Germany, and West Berlin as the eleventh state of West Germany—West Berlin had become an island, a city-state enclosed by a perimeter wall and surrounded by a hostile territory. Because of this captivity, West Berlin had not recuperated from its postwar crisis. The city still contained vast tracts of empty space in which buildings seemed to be isolated islands and, in the 1970s, its population was declining.

In 1977 a group of architects launched a rescue project called Berlin as a Green Archipelago. Led by Oswald Mathias Ungers, the group included Rem Koolhaas, Peter Riemann, Hans Kollhoff, and Arthur Ovaska. To these architects, the problems of postwar West Berlin provided a potent model of "cities within the city," or in Ungers's terms, a "city made by islands."[1] This approach reflected the driving concept of Ungers's urban projects, which he and his students elaborated between 1964 and 1977, first when he was first teaching at the Technical University in Berlin (1963–1969) and then at Cornell University (1968–1986).[2] Ungers sought to turn Berlin's idiosyncratic character as a politically divided city in economic difficulty into a laboratory for a project of the city that countered the technocratic and romantic approaches popular at the time. Berlin as a Green Archipelago can also be understood as one of the earliest critiques of the Krier brothers' perimeter block restorations, which would have a decisive impact on the reconstruction of Berlin in the 1980s and 1990s.[3]

Berlin's fragmented reality—a city whose ruins registered the destruction of war, yet whose political intensity reflected its position as the "capital" of the Cold War—provided Ungers with a basis for interpreting the city as an entity no longer reliant on large-scale urban planning but rather composed of islands, each of which was conceived as a formally distinct micro-city. Ungers derived this approach from Karl Friedrich Schinkel, who was the city architect of Berlin during the first half of the nineteenth century. Schinkel had envisioned the capital of Prussia as a fabric punctuated by singular architectural interventions, rather than as a city planned along the principles of cohesive spatial design typical of the baroque period. For Ungers, this approach could overcome the fragmentation of postwar Berlin by turning the crisis itself (the impossibility of planning the city) into the very project of the *architecture of the city*. Following this line of thinking, Ungers developed his theory of the city as an archipelago, shrinking the city to points of urban density as a way to respond to the dramatic drop in West Berlin's population.

Berlin as a Green Archipelago is one of the very few projects in the history of city planning to address an urban crisis by radically shifting the focus from the problem of urbanization—the further growth of the city—to that of shrinking the city. Ungers's archipelago looked to frame and thus to form the existing city by accepting its process of depopulation. This acceptance was not projected as a "disurbanization" of the city, but as a way to

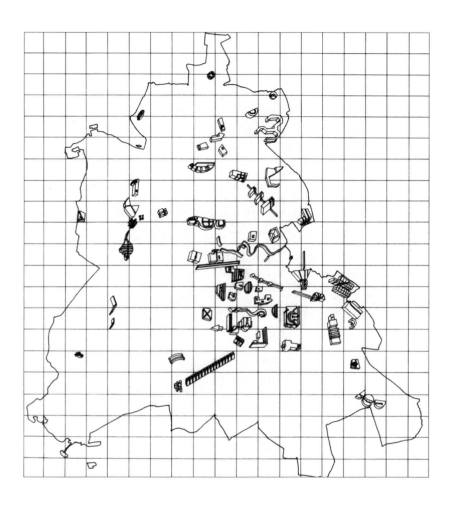

5.1
Oswald Mathias Ungers, Rem Koolhaas, Hans Kollhoff,
Arthur Ovaska, and Peter Riemann, The City within the
City—Berlin as a Green Archipelago, 1977. The city
as a "project of crisis," shrinking the city to its significant
and irreducible parts.

reinforce its form by articulating the limits of each "island" in an archipelago of large-scale artifacts.

Countering the utopian visions of city dissolution or, conversely, the ideal of reducing the city to an overall system, or even of restoring the image of urban control by consolidating forms such as the perimeter block, Berlin as a Green Archipelago proposed a paradigm that went beyond modernist and postmodernist references and that even today is not fully appreciated for its provocative logic. This logic is revealed by tracing the development of Ungers's project of the city through the series of proposals and studies he worked on in the 1960s and 1970s. This series can be seen as *one* project culminating in Berlin as a Green Archipelago, especially when one considers Ungers's seminal urban design projects, his didactic research on Berlin, and then the link between his work and theories and OMA's early attempt to define a "metropolitan architecture." The intellectual exchange between Ungers and OMA was one of the most interesting lines of research about the city in the 1970s, even if it was not sufficiently developed. This exchange was based not only on the collaboration between Koolhaas and Ungers on key projects, but also on their mutual interest in the development of a "third way" to address the project of the city. Both sought to move beyond the impasse represented by modernist city planning and the incipient postmodern deconstruction of any project of the city.

The central focus of this chapter is to reconstruct Ungers's project as an attempt to define the architecture of the city as invested in architectural form. In his projects, Ungers articulated the limits and finitude of architectural form as possible "cities within the city," as a recovery of defining traits of the city, such as its inherent collective dimension, its dialectical nature, its being made of separate parts, its being a composition of different and at time opposing forms, within the urban crisis that was affecting many cities in the late 1960s and 1970s, of which Berlin was the most extreme and thus paradigmatic example.

Ungers's formation as an architect coincided with one of the most difficult periods of German history. After the Second World War, Germans faced not only the task of rebuilding a country devastated by war, but also the tormented political, cultural, and moral reconstruction of a nation that for twelve years had succumbed to Nazism. Reconstruction was also difficult because Germany was the epicenter of Cold War politics. The ideological contraposition of East and West charged the reconstruction with ideological momentum, which produced on both sides, via a series of plans and competitions, exemplary urban projects whose forms and programs resonated as models for other cities throughout Germany and Europe.[4] Two of the most exemplary flagship projects were the Stalinallee in the East, a monumental boulevard planned in 1952 by Hermann Henselmann and completed in 1960 as the new center of East Berlin, capital of East Germany, and the Hansa Viertel Interbau in the West, a residential district planned in 1957 and completed in 1961 as an international exhibition of housing projects designed by key figures in modern architecture, including Alvar Aalto, Walter Gropius, and Oscar Niemeyer. Besides emphasizing the dialectical nature of city, the formal and ideological contraposition of these projects also made explicit the impasse in defining new models for city reconstruction. If the Stalinallee recuperated, with monumental emphasis, the theme of the boulevard as the main image of the city, the Hansa Viertel produced the opposite extreme with an image of scattered housing types in a green landscape. It may have been the search for a third way, beyond these two directions, that motivated Ungers's early attempts to outline his principles for the project of the city.

These principles were first formulated in a series of urban projects that Ungers developed in the early 1960s: housing proposals for Cologne Neue Stadt (1961–1964), Cologne Grünzug Süd (1962–1965), and Berlin Märkisches Viertel (1962–1967), and a competition entry for a student dormitory in Enschede, Holland (1964). Ungers's approach in these projects was explicitly polemical. Their rational, monumental form was intended as a critique of the late modernist praxis of designing the city through the generic application of given building standards, which reduced the role of the architect to the design of envelopes. In opposition to the traditional mandate given to urban projects, the main principle guiding these proposals was the conception of new housing complexes not as a generic extension of the city but as clearly formalized *city parts*, as finite artifacts that, in their internal formal composition, were evocative of an idea of the city.

The project for Cologne Neue Stadt, for example, was a direct critique of a typical late-modernist urban layout in which slabs and towers were scattered in green areas without producing a recognizable form. Ungers's complex was conceived as a series of residential towers of different heights, yet composed to form a single architectural entity. The typical plan of each apartment placed discrete rooms around the main living space. This composition gave form to the towers themselves, which were grouped vertical volumes that further articulated the spatial and formal composition of the entire complex. With this inventive composition, Ungers elevated the living room from just another room in the apartment to a sort of atrium (eliminating the corridor), while defining the exterior form of the housing blocks as a monumental composition of volumes. Alluding to the play of light and shadow produced by such an idiosyncratic formal composition, Ungers defined his Neue Stadt project as the archetype for a city of "negatives and positives"—that is, a city in which the

5.2
Oswald Mathias Ungers, proposal for Neue Stadt
Housing Complex, Cologne, 1961–1964. The city as
a composition of "positives and negatives."

experience of form as a composition of built and void space became the main architectural motif.⁵

This solution was Ungers's first attempt to incorporate within an architectural complex the spatial phenomenology of the city. He applied the same approach, albeit less successfully, to the Märkisches Viertel complex in Berlin, grouping the given program of residential towers to form a sequence of open courts with irregular forms. As in Neue Stadt, he proposed to alter the given distribution of the apartments by changing the form or position of one or two rooms in each column of apartments. This procedure created a formal tension between the simplicity of each architectural part and the complexity of spatial arrangements created by their overall composition. This tension can be interpreted as an implicit critique of the spatial monotony of postwar urban settlements. In both Neue Stadt and Märkisches Viertel, Ungers accepted the building technology and typological standards that were given for these housing complexes, but he altered their formal composition in order to recuperate the possibility of monumental form within the peripheral spaces in which they were inserted.

Such a critique of postwar urbanism is explicit in Ungers's project for the Enschede student housing competition in Holland. He designed this complex as a catalog of formal compositions starting with the basic figures of geometry—the triangle, the square, and the circle. Similar to his previous schemes, the design method produced a complex space evocative of the city by using a very restricted formal vocabulary. In reaction to the site—on the outskirts of a provincial town—Ungers rejected the typical settlement logic of a campus of scattered pavilions in a green space and proposed to design the new campus addition in the form of a self-sufficient city, whose spatiality recalls the complex composition of spaces of Hadrian's villa, but whose

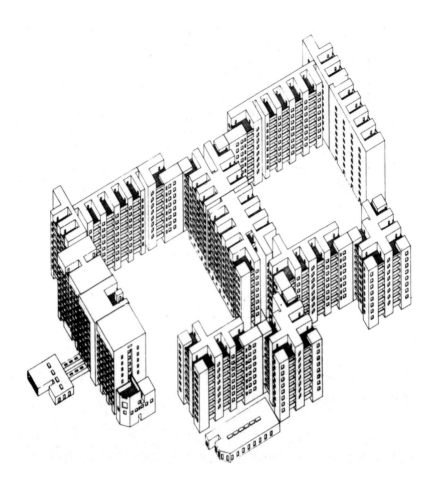

5.3
Oswald Mathias Ungers, Märkisches Viertel Housing
Complex, Berlin, 1962–1967, axonometric. The
project achieves a sense of monumentality through
the use of raw, prefabricated architectural forms.

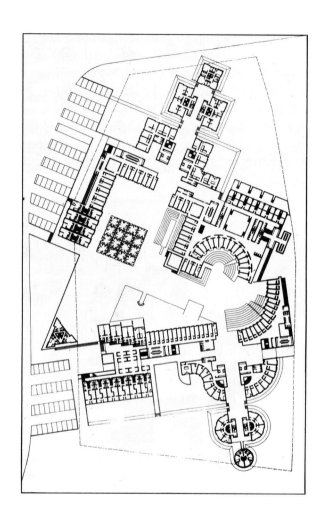

5.4
Oswald Mathias Ungers, competition entry for a
student dormitory, Enschede, Holland, 1964. Plan of
the complex. An example of *coincidentia oppositorum*:
mixing Durand's normative architecture with the
spatial complexity of Hadrian's villa.

building forms are reminiscent of Jean-Nicolas-Louis Durand's austere architectural grammar.

The articulation of simple architectural volumes to compose and frame complex sequences of spaces assumes a radical form in what can be considered Ungers's canonical urban design project: Cologne Grünzug Süd. While the idiosyncratic composition of volumes for Neue Stadt, Märkisches Viertel, and Enschede critiqued the repetitive spatial patterns of modernist town planning, the proposal for a residential district at Grünzug Süd (which he presented at the Team Ten meeting in Berlin in 1966)[6] can be seen as Ungers's critique of one of the most emblematic alternatives to late-modernist urban design: the megastructure.

At the time of the project, Grünzug Süd was a suburb with no outstanding urban or architectural features. The initial reason for remodeling the area was that the newly built Autobahn connected the city's ring road to Bonn. Instead of designing a new complex like Neue Stadt or Märkisches Viertel, Ungers conceived the project as a gradual transformation of the site based on a systematic morphological rereading of its somewhat ordinary form. Ungers took the direction of the area's main street as a section through which to analyze the morphology of the city. Following this analysis, he evolved the city's existing, heterogeneous collection of spaces and buildings into a linear composition of clearly defined, different architectural events made by different building typologies.[7]

This approach did not rely on mimetic contextualism, however, but adopted a vocabulary of abstract and austere architectural forms. What Ungers extrapolated from the existing city fabric were not its vernacular or iconographic elements, but rather the most abstract architectural elements found in the sequence of open and closed spaces, the rhythms of walls, the volumetric effects of firewalls, and the seriality of housing facades with their

Bauformen, Gebäudeordnungen und Themen
der Umgebung

1  2  3

  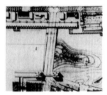

Spalte 1: Einfamilienhausreihe: Addition glei-
cher Elemente. Wechsel zwischen geschlosse-
ner, formulierter und offener, unformulierter
Zone

Spalte 2: Durchgebildete, unterschiedliche Ein-
zelkörper vor zusammenfassender Wand

Spalte 3: Tor und Brücke

188

Spalte 4: Geschichtete Baukörper zwischen Wänden

Spalte 5: a) Straßenraum, b) horizontale Baukörper mit vertikaler Durchdringung

Spalte 6: Platz mit eingestellten Objekten

5.5

Oswald Mathias Ungers, competition entry for Grünzug
Süd, 1962, as presented in *Deutsche Bauzeitung* 7
(1966). Against the megastructure: city form as a
(linear) composition of parts. The intervention uncovers
the latent formal themes of the existing city.

repetitive patterns of openings. These formal elements were transformed into austere compositions of new housing, through which the site's latent urban text was made explicit and legible: for example, the linear form of the fragmented existing row houses was recombined in the variegated rhythm of the new houses.

This strategy is illustrated in a presentation panel of the project in which the entire plan of Grünzug Süd is framed as a linear composition of six distinct parts.[8] Each part is further illustrated not with a rendering of the new interventions, but with photographs of the existing elements. The photographs depict ordinary spatial situations—street views, interrupted rows of buildings, firewalls, passages, open fields—and render the spatial discontinuity of the city as the main architectural form of the project. The formal tension between the extant and the new suggests more than an acknowledgment of the existing situation as a starting point for the project; it also shows the constitutive formal tension of city form: the dialectic between the irreducible formal and spatial autonomy of each part and the possibility of conceiving the different parts as one coherent structure, as a *city part*. In Grünzug Süd this dialectical tension is deliberately radicalized.

While the formal coherence imposed by the megastructure subsumed the entire city within a single "structure" that could expand ad infinitum, the linear composition of Grünzug Süd not only presupposed the city as a dialectical composition of large, yet limited artifacts, but also considered the internal structure of these artifacts as separate and autonomous parts. This internal structure reflected the separateness that characterizes city form and became, in its limited dimension, a representation of the city. As the project's realism demonstrated, Ungers's "city within the city" was not the creation of an idyllic village as opposed to the fragmentation of the city, but an attempt to reflect the splintering form of the city from within the architectural artifact itself.

Grünzug Süd was not built, but it provided the ideas that became the basis of his studies on Berlin.

Between 1963 and 1969 Ungers taught at the Technical University of Berlin. Prior to his arrival, conventional student assignments were based on ideal programs such as "a house for an artist" or "a house near a lake," and were devoid of any urban implication.[9] To counter this clear separation of architecture and urban design, Ungers introduced design experiments based on a systematic reading of the city, and proposed to make West Berlin a laboratory for architectural speculation. The most critical conditions, such as the city's insularity, postwar fragmentation, uneven urban development, and the Berlin Wall, would be mapped and turned into a field of possibilities for radical architectural inventions.

This approach was a polemical stance against Hans Scharoun's influence on the culture of the school.[10] During the 1950s Scharoun had worked on a planning idea for Berlin that culminated in his entry for the international Berlin Hauptstadt competition (1958). Scharoun proposed transforming the entire city into a vast green park served by an efficient web of motorways. The project opposed the monumentality of East Berlin's urban interventions, such as the Stalinallee, as well as the historical legacy of Prussian Berlin, which Scharoun identified as the progenitor of Nazi ideology. Working against these legacies, Scharoun projected the destruction of Berlin as the possibility of an anticity, a disurbanist plan in which the ruins of Berlin were turned into a utopian pastoral scene.

Opposing this interpretation of the city, Ungers saw Berlin in its most critical form—a divided city composed of irreducibly divergent parts and, because of the uncertainty of its reconstruction, in a state of permanent incompletion. Ungers found an archetype for this situation in Schinkel's projects for the so-called Havellandschaft (the landscape around the river Havel), a vast complex of pavilions, castles, and gardens that Schinkel, together with his collaborators and Peter Joseph Lenné, developed throughout the first half of the nineteenth century as a royal amenity for the Hohenzollern.[11] Commissioned by the royal family to design a sort of Hadrian's villa to be built along the Havel, Schinkel had proposed a landscape of architectural events that involved the entire area of the river without subsuming it within an overall geometrical composition. His interventions took the form of an archipelago in which architecture was juxtaposed with the natural setting. The paradigm for Ungers's later approach was one of the Havellandschaft sites: Schinkel's design for Klein Glienicke, a garden with pavilions designed between 1824 and 1837, which Ungers would use as a veritable guiding archetype for himself and his students on the essential nature of Berlin. In this complex, architectural objects such as a casino, villa, and pavilion are placed in the garden without any axial reference; rather, they establish unexpected relationships that are further multiplied by other, smaller architectural elements scattered within the park. What characterizes Klein Glienicke is the radical opposition between the richness of the spatial relationships and the elemental simplicity of the architecture made of primary forms, such as the pergola on the Havel. Moreover, these forms are not just fragments scattered in the park. Because of their different compositions, materials, and programs, they are all based on a formal grammar that establishes an archipelago of formal events. Schinkel used the same approach in his interventions in Berlin. The city's fabric, fragmented after the urban crisis of the Napoleonic war, was not corrected with attempts to produce overall plans but was simply assumed to be the landscape of the city. Schinkel developed his public works as point compositions of autonomous blocks freely arranged within the space of the city, leaving the incompleteness of the urban fabric as the possibility for a new spatiality. Ungers adapted this conception of Berlin in order to address the effects of war on the city rather than tap into a romantic ideal. In this context, Schinkel's open compositions along the Havel and in Berlin were used to sublimate the fragmented landscape of contemporary Berlin.

Following this reading of the city and employing the method Ungers used for Grünzug Süd, his students produced systematic morphological and geographic surveys of Berlin in which they systematically analyzed the infrastructure of the city—the Autobahn, the parks, the canals, the river Spree, the U-Bahn network.[12] These layers of Berlin were viewed not only as urban data, but also in terms of their architectural consequences: as disruptive forms that divided the city into parts, obstructing any organic recovery of the city. The unpredictable way in which the river Spree cut through the city, for example, was assumed to be the logic for settlement interventions that would transform the disrupted sites into parts of a new linear city.[13] Rather than trying to "solve" the crises of the city, the projects proposed with this method sought to exploit them as the thematic form of the project itself. Looking at the projects shown in Ungers's course booklets, one sees the contrast between the will to contextualize the project themes and interventions in the most critical points of the city and the will to confront these conditions with an austere repertoire of restrained forms. In one project, published in *Wohnen am Park* (Buildings in the park), four partially destroyed city blocks are superimposed on a sequence of three different residential structures (a mixed-use slab, a low-rise T-shaped building, and a mixed-use courtyard building), all held together in a linear composition by a public elevated street.[14] While the elevated street unites the four blocks in one complex, the three proposed freestanding buildings fill the blocks without completing their perimeters, thus maintaining the status of ruins in the "park" of the complex. The common basis for all of these projects was point interventions: instead of being made with an overall plan, the project for Berlin was made through the design of radical urban architectures that envisioned the development of the city as the eruption of radical forms of metropolitan living. In some cases the students simply mapped existing "ordinary" features of the city and idealized them not as default situations but as explicit projects. For example, the numerous firewalls made visible by the destruction of the war were systematically photographed and then compiled to create an architectural sequence of blind brick walls that also parodied the Berlin Wall.[15]

The best representation of this method came not from Berlin but from London. In the late 1960s, chafing against Archigram's dominant pedagogy at the Architectural Association, Elia Zenghelis, a teacher at the AA, introduced the students in his unit, among them Rem Koolhaas, to Ungers's work. In a conversation with Ungers in 2004, Koolhaas said that Grünzug Süd was his first contact with Ungers's work.[16]

In 1971, Koolhaas decided to visit the Berlin Wall and document it as a work of architecture for his third-year project.[17] Koolhaas's description of the architecture of the wall is similar to Ungers's compositional logic for Grünzug Süd. Koolhaas discusses his discovery that the linear structure of the wall was not just a single line cutting through the city, but a linear sequence of different architectural events held together by the political will to impose on the city a state of closure.[18] In his description, Koolhaas strategically silences the political meaning of the wall to emphasize the way in which the political institution of closure, once made real within the form of the city, manifested itself not as the ideal form of a line, but in the ordinary forms

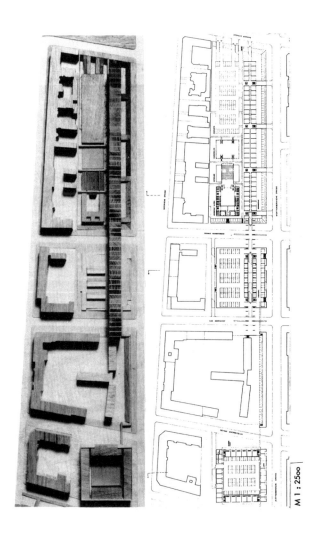

5.6
Ulrike Bangerter, multifunctional block, ground-floor
plan and model, from *Wohnen am Park*, 1967, student
project no. 5.

of houses, walls, fences, and other architectural means of the division of space.

It was precisely the "ordinary" architecture of the Berlin Wall that suggested to Koolhaas how even the most imposing artifact, once deployed in a real situation, loses its purity as a unitary form and becomes a sequence of very different situations. Following Ungers's Grünzug Süd project and the "retroactive" rationalization of existing critical situations that Ungers and his students applied in their projects for Berlin, Koolhaas "elevated" the Berlin Wall as a representation of how architecture was more likely to provoke discontinuity than unity. This is evident in the pictures of the wall that Koolhaas used in order to construct his argument. In these photos, the linear form of the wall, like the strip of Grünzug Süd, becomes many different spatial events—open fields, rows of buildings, fences made of different materials, etc. As in the projects of Ungers's students, the theme of the wall is represented through a series of radically different situations hardly conceivable as a coherent sequence or form of continuity, but instead revealing city form as a site of radical discontinuity.[19]

One can argue that such an approach to the city—an approach inspired by Ungers's Grünzug Süd project—became the conceptual basis for Koolhaas's *Delirious New York*, which uses the most critical urban conditions as the basis for a city project.[20] In following this link between Ungers and the early work of Koolhaas and Zenghelis, we can see the fundamental development of Ungers's city-within-the-city concept as the germ of Koolhaas and Zenghelis's Exodus, or the Voluntary Prisoners of Architecture (1972). As the subtitle suggests, the subject of this project is the inmate. Koolhaas and Zenghelis intended the "voluntary prisoner" to serve as a metaphor for the inhabitant of the metropolis in its most extreme condition, an exacerbated version of communitarian citizenship based on self-imposed closure.[21] The voluntary prisoner is a metaphor for a subject who deliberately accepts the reality of the city as made of separation and exclusion rather than unity and inclusion. Correspondingly, Exodus consists of two parallel walls cutting through London and dividing it into eight enclosed parts. Both the housing complex of Grünzug Süd and the Berlin Wall also cut through an existing city, encompassing and radicalizing the different city conditions. Exodus was not simply a line, like Superstudio's Continuous Monument, or the repetition of an identical module, like Ivan Leonidov's scheme for Magnitogorsk (although both projects were surely inspirations for Exodus); it was a linear composition made of radically different city parts. Each of these parts was meant to be a morphological and programmatic exaggeration of city parts (the suburb, the hospital, the museum, the park) in the form of social and architectural allegories of city life. Exodus deliberately assumed that conditions such as separation, aggression, and enmity were logical ingredients for the city. Thus, Exodus evolved from Ungers's interpretation of Berlin as a city made of contrasting parts to a more explicit political scenario.

In a recent lecture, Zenghelis maintained that the different parts of Exodus were conceived in two ways: as arranged within a linear structure, and as autonomous city islands for independent metropolitan communities.[22] As a project, Exodus—for which Ungers, after encountering Koolhaas, showed great admiration and interest—can be considered the link connecting the architectural principles introduced in Grünzug Süd and Ungers's studies on Berlin with the more politically explicit project of Berlin as a Green Archipelago. For Exodus amplified a theme already emergent in Ungers's work: the principle of turning the splintering forces of the metropolis into architectural form that addresses the collective dimension of the city.

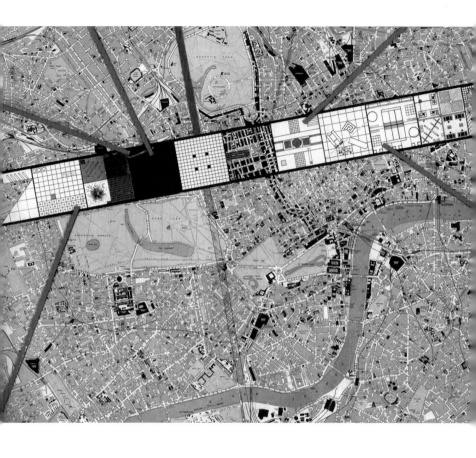

5.7
Rem Koolhaas and Elia Zenghelis with Madelon
Vriesendorp and Zoe Zenghelis, Exodus, or the
Voluntary Prisoners of Architecture, 1972, plan.
Architectural form as analogous to the splintering
forms of the metropolis.

Ungers had already begun to elaborate a more overtly political approach in the research topics he initiated upon moving to the United States in 1969. (For one year, 1968–1969, he taught both in Berlin and at Cornell.) Living in upstate New York, he became interested in historical examples of communal life in America, and wrote a book on this topic with his wife, Liselotte, in the early 1970s.[23] It is easy to imagine that Ungers began to research these communities for possible social and political clues that would support his idea of the city as a field of delimited forms. Countering the traditional Marxist critique of experimental socialist communes as irrelevant in changing the general organization of society, Ungers argued that these American communities provided a viable urban paradigm.

For example, in an essay summarizing his studies of religious communities, Ungers considered how radical social lifestyles were implemented not only as totalizing utopias imposed on the whole of society, but also as a set of communitarian principles voluntarily embraced by secessionist groups that built their villages as self-sufficient places, independent from existing urban centers.[24] According to Ungers, these "concrete utopias" were possible precisely because they were conceived as limited in terms of space and number of inhabitants. Religious communities such as the Shakers were characterized by a principle of communal life in which there was no private property; all facilities were for collective use. This resulted in settlements whose form was organized for a communal life, with an abundance of common spaces, and in clear contrast to cities, which are shaped by land ownership. Ungers observed that radical communality was possible only within limited settlements, where an increase in population did not result in the growth of individual settlements but in their multiplication. The limits of each settlement were self-imposed by the community itself according to the possibility of self-management; thus their form was independent from any external urban order.

These villages were not the embodiment of economic segregation or other social management criteria, but of the ideological will of a community to separate itself from the rest of society by following a principle of collective life. This example led Ungers to believe that developing an idea of the city as an archipelago of limited parts was more feasible than attempting to realize overall projects like those of modernist architects; in addition, the concept of the archipelago opened up a new political conception of a city form in which groups of inhabitants could self-organize their independence through architectural artifacts that allowed them to claim space for their communitarian life.

A similar observation emerged in Ungers's research on the superblock. He especially focused on the Vienna superblock, the most prominent urban architectural project of the social-democratic government of the Austrian capital between 1919 and 1934. The so-called Red Vienna can be considered the clearest representation of what a "city within the city" means, and is thus one of the most important references for Berlin as a Green Archipelago. Over the course of a few years, and in spite of difficult economic circumstances, the government of Vienna had constructed 14,000 new apartments for the working class in the form of blocks located within the city. In one of his course booklets Ungers published a map of the Viennese superblocks, which showed that their locations were not based on an overall city plan but were point interventions.[25] The municipality proposed locating these new housing schemes within the city, counter to an initial idea of building them on the periphery as an extension of the city. In an introductory article to his research on the Vienna superblock, Ungers stressed how this typology was an alternative to the settlement logic of both the garden city and the

Siedlung; in those models, the working class was alienated from the rest of society within a fragmented and marginalized district on the periphery of industrial cities. Vienna's municipal government opted instead for a new social housing stock in the form of a very precise typology: the Hof, a superblock whose spatial and programmatic principle was based on monumental interior courtyards reminiscent of the monastic typology of the cloister. Ungers noted that the main goal of the Vienna government was to raise working-class consciousness and the communitarian spirit of its inhabitants rather than just to solve the problem of a housing shortage. For this reason, the Viennese superblocks did not expand the existing city, but were situated within the city as self-sufficient islands in pronounced contrast to their surroundings. As Ungers emphasized, the superblock's clear architectural identity and generosity of collective spaces were in opposition to the individualization of bourgeois metropolitan residences. Unlike many modernist city projects, the Viennese superblocks were not innovative in terms of style, newness of building components, or layout of the apartments; instead, their innovation lay in their radical redistribution of collective facilities within a radical and recognizable architectural form. Each superblock was equipped with basic community services such as a clinic, library, laundry, gym, restaurant, and kindergarten. These facilities were designed to provide the superblock with both self-sufficiency and a monumental character that was intended to convey the political image of these complexes through the use of their collective spaces. The result was the autonomy of the superblocks from the planning standards of the city, which led to an archipelago of places for communitarian life. The formal and typological theme of the courtyard was decisive in reinforcing the identity of this communitarian life.

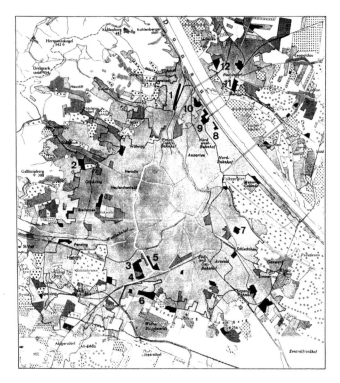

5.8
Map of Red Vienna, from Oswald Mathias Ungers,
Die Wiener Superblocks (1969). The city as
an archipelago of large-scale housing blocks.

5.9
Karl Ehn, Karl-Marx-Hof, Vienna, 1926–1931.
View of the courtyard showing gardens, kindergarten,
and arched pavilions.

This aspect was also decisive in Ungers's reevaluation of the superblock. He stressed that while modernist planning focused on refining architectural space with optimal living standards, the architects of the superblocks focused instead on the thematic performance of space, giving the architecture a precise ritual identity that would elevate social housing from the mere act of providing space for the social management of the working class to the bold gesture of a monumentality that gave the inhabitants dignity without masking their class identity. Ungers's fascination with both the communes of America and the idea of the super-block as a building type, which corresponded to his idea of the city as a composition of *Grossform* (big form), added a social and political dimension to the concept of designing a city through the kinds of point interventions that he took from Schinkel's Berlin.

This increasingly political understanding of the city as archi-pelago was triggered by two events: one, Ungers's encounter with Koolhaas and Zenghelis in 1972, and the other, his confrontation with Colin Rowe's "neoliberal" theory of urban design, which took form in the early 1970s as *Collage City*. For Ungers, the latter event was decisive in clarifying that his concept of the city as an archipelago was more than just the morphological collage of dif-ferent architectural figures.

Rowe first invited Ungers to teach at Cornell in 1968. As his academic and professional position became increasingly con-troversial with the anti-architecture political protests in German universities in 1968, Ungers moved to Cornell in hope of find-ing a more sympathetic university environment.[26] At the time, Rowe was shifting his work from a close reading of architecture to the formulation of a comprehensive theory of urban design, which would later appear in his book *Collage City* (published in 1978, but completed in 1973).[27] Rowe countered the utopian ta-bula rasa method of modernist planning with an urbanism based on a sophisticated bricolage of different historical architectural examples. Such an approach, he held, would lead to a city fit for a liberal democratic regime based on the cultural principles of inclusion and pluralism. For Rowe, the formal paradigm for such an ideal city was already realized in the Rome depicted by Giovanni Battista Nolli in his famous topographic survey.[28] Through the ideological lens of liberal politics, Rowe transformed Nolli's Rome into a "collage city," a city formed by the incremental adjustment of disparate architectural forms, yielding an intricate collage of elegant architectural "figures" coexisting, in spite of their differences, within the "ground" of the city fabric. By this move, Rowe compressed Rome's time-based evolution into the present tense, suppressing its heritage of conflict by collapsing its complexity into a single temporal layer. The potential for conflict was reduced to mere morphological variety contained within the informal framework of the topographic ground—the city's irregular fabric—which in Rowe's terms was meant to act as a poché between the different figures.

Rowe invited Ungers to Cornell because he assumed that Ungers's ideas in architecture and urban design were evolving in a direction similar to his bricolage approach. But it was precisely Ungers's recognition of the fundamental difference between Rowe's project and his own that helped him to further radicalize the theoretical premises of his approach, which he later characterized as the "dialectic city," as opposed to Rowe's "collage city."[29]

Rowe's central thesis in *Collage City* revolves around understanding architecture as offering "set pieces" for building city spaces. Set pieces are architectural forms that can be reduced to relativistic devices freely extrapolated from any historical, political, or geographical context. The only context Rowe acknowledges is morphological collage: the possibility of combining radically different architectural figures in a pleasant composition.

According to him, any architectural figure can sustain multiple uses as long as it remains useful and convincing as a figure—namely, as a morphological datum. Rowe argues that its convincingness as a figure is merely based on the architect's personal sense of morphology. The criteria of composition, by implication, are subjective and separated from the broader cultural and political context, which Ungers placed at the center of his idea of the city of contrasting parts. In Rowe's idea of the city, difference is reduced to a mere morphological exercise: the incremental accumulation of differences. It was precisely against this idea of urban design that Ungers developed his own method. Ungers's rejection of this image of the city of accumulation, the concrete result of free-market politics, becomes evident in what can be considered the two most important projects he elaborated in the 1970s, during his American period: the urban design proposals for two areas of West Berlin—Tiergarten Viertel and Lichterfelde.

The project for Tiergarten Viertel was Ungers's competition entry for the area around West Berlin's cultural center, the Kulturforum, developed in the 1960s as the city's ideological counterpart to the East's Alexanderplatz.[30] The Kulturforum was already a place of conflicting ideologies, as it consisted of two radically different buildings: Scharoun's expressionist Philharmonic Concert Hall and Public Library, and Mies van der Rohe's classicist New National Gallery. The dialectic between Scharoun's and Mies's interventions was more than a stylistic one, as it summarized the two most important cultural directions that had animated Germany in the first half of the twentieth century: expressionism and rationalism. At the time of the competition, the area was in a fragmented state, and the resolutely insular form of Mies's National Gallery was perhaps the most appropriate comment.

The competition called for a densification and recomposition of the area's fragmented urban structure. Ungers rejected

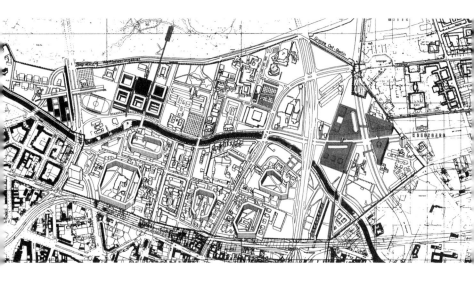

5.10
Oswald Mathias Ungers, proposal for the Tiergarten
Viertel, Berlin 1973, axonometric. Fusing architectural
abstraction and urban realism.

the idea of recomposition, and instead highlighted the existing condition in order to transform fragmentation into a contrasting composition of forms. Instead of solving the project within one overall scheme, he articulated his plan in six different and autonomous architectural artifacts that responded to local situations. These artifacts were imagined as superblocks loosely gathered along the Landwehrkanal, the small river that framed the southern part of the Kulturforum. Each superblock contained a mixed-use program (housing, offices, shops, hotels, community facilities). Reminiscent of Durand's and Superstudio's gridded architectural compositions, the architecture was radically abstract and generic, made by extruding simple archetypes such as a square, a cruciform, and a perimeter block. The clear reference to Superstudio can be interpreted as reflecting Koolhaas's influence on this stage of Ungers's work.[31] In the Tiergarten Viertel project, Superstudio's Continuous Monument was interpreted as a sequence of artifacts made from the same gridded volumes that the Florentine group called "histograms of architecture." According to Superstudio, the histograms were the expression of a radically generic and imageless architecture indifferent to program and context. Ungers appropriated Superstudio's histograms as the most suitable language vis-à-vis the programmatic instability that characterized the superblocks, yet he inflected their abstract form according to the conditions of the site. While Rowe's set pieces were quotations of the historical city, Ungers's city forms were generic yet responsive to existing situations, especially those that had no historical pedigree, such as traffic intersections, wastelands, and incomplete perimeter blocks. In the proposal, extremely repetitive eight-story courtyard buildings were inserted into existing fragmented perimeter blocks to create a contrast between the fragmented perimeter and the continuity of the new block. A wasteland is colonized with six equal blocks clustered into one form in order not to completely spoil the empty area. An underground block is inserted within Mies's and Scharoun's civic monuments in the form of a "negative" block that functions as a metro station. Unlike Rowe's value-free figurative exuberance, these interventions were each spatially different yet made with the same formal grammar: simple orthogonal extrusions of built form. In this way, difference was not an ad hoc accumulation of architectures, but the dialectical tension between different city spaces—the courtyard, the block, the sunken plaza—produced by the juxtaposition of simple forms.

In this sense Ungers's approach is much closer to Peter and Alison Smithson's "as-found" method than to Rowe's collage. Since the 1950s, the Smithsons' as-found approach to the city consisted of fine-tuning modern architecture's formal achievements with the concrete conditions of the postwar contemporary city, such as fragmentation, mass culture, and the anonymity of the urban landscape. While many architects took inspiration from the ordinary and the everyday image of the city, what characterized the as-found was the Smithsons' commitment to the language of modern architecture. This approach was eloquently elaborated in their late 1970s book, *Without Rhetoric*, in which they attempt to rewrite modern architectural examples as pragmatic solutions to the city's most contemporary problems rather than as idealistic projections.[32] Peter Smithson first presented this position at Ungers's seminars in Berlin in the late 1960s.[33] A "without rhetoric" approach is evident in Ungers's projects of that period, and especially in his competition entry for a housing district in Lichterfelde, which, together with Tiergarten Viertel, represented Ungers's most radical step toward the idea of the city that he would summarize in Berlin as a Green Archipelago.[34]

Lichterfelde is an ordinary suburb comprising single-family houses and apartment blocks. In 1973, there was a proposal to connect this suburb to other parts of the city with a new ring road, which gave rise to a competition for a new residential settlement. In his entry, Ungers proposed to articulate the new settlement in the form of a barcode organized perpendicularly to the proposed vehicular artery. Even though the barcode form was a clear revisitation of the modernist *Siedlung* of parallel rows of buildings, the rows here were made not just of continuous buildings but of a heterogeneous sequence of typologies, especially unheroic types such as urban villas and low-rise row houses. Ungers chose these typologies because they were already present in the site. The project systematically cataloged existing ordinary features of the site, such as individual houses, small pathways, rows of trees, and semipublic gardens. Ungers proposed to reorganize and alter these "found" features according to the linear logic of the barcode, which strengthened the form of the settlement by organizing these features in strips.[35] In this way, the existing quasi-suburban condition of the city was gradually transformed into a coherent and abstract architectural composition without altering the attributes of the original situation. As in Tiergarten Viertel, the as-found conditions of the site are accepted and even assumed to be the guiding principle of the city, yet they are framed and organized by an abstract form—in the case of Lichterfelde, with the strips.

Ungers's formal operations constituted another fundamental aspect of these projects, besides establishing a further crucial difference from Rowe's *Collage City*. These operations on form were rooted in the analysis of the collective nature of the city: its common, ordinary, collective forms, rather than its individual architectural figures. In projects such as Tiergarten Viertel and Lichterfelde, the design intervention consists of the formation of city parts around contemporary forms of public and collective spaces. The spaces—like the kitchen gardens of Grünzug Süd

5.11
Oswald Mathias Ungers, Rem Koolhaas, and
Karl Dietzch, competition entry for IV Ring,
Berlin-Lichterfelde, Berlin, 1974, plan.

and Lichterfelde, the sunken metro station, or the sport center in Tiergarten Viertel—are not camouflaged with the traditional spatial and symbolic attributes of publicness such as plazas and monuments, but are rendered in all their metropolitan anonymity.

Like Schinkel's approach to Berlin, Ungers's urban design proposals deliberately accepted and made visible the effects of forces on the city such as the fragmentation of urban form, anonymity of architecture, and instability of program. Projects such as Tiergarten Viertel, Lichterfelde, and those made by Ungers's students all attempted to extract from these urban forces the seeds for the architectural reinvention of the city as a site of contrasting collective forms. It is in light of this attitude, which mixed urban realism and what one might call the "will to city form," that OMA's early work can be considered part of the development of ideas and projects that would lead Ungers toward Berlin as a Green Archipelago.

Koolhaas worked with Ungers on both the Tiergarten Viertel and Lichterfelde projects, and OMA's early projects were carried out in close dialog with Ungers, whose initials—OMU—were an inspiration for the name of Koolhaas and Zenghelis's office.[36] In 1972, after completing Exodus, Koolhaas moved to Ithaca, New York, to study at Cornell with Rowe and Ungers. He immediately realized there were differences between the two men's approaches, and that his own position had much more affinity with Ungers's explicit adherence to the reality of the city than with Rowe's nostalgic approach.[37] When Koolhaas met Ungers, the German architect was conducting research with his students on idiosyncratic urban forms of the American city as models for new urban design interventions. It was in this context that Koolhaas began his research for his book *Delirious New York*.[38] The narrative structure of *Delirious New York* is itself organized as a kind of "archipelago" in which New York is analyzed not through the isotropic order of the grid but through the individuality of exemplary artifacts such as Rockefeller Center, the RCA Building, the Downtown Athletic Club, and the Waldorf-Astoria Hotel. Koolhaas identified the potential of these architectures as "cities within cities,"[39] microcosms in which the metropolitan life of New York was contained and its social and ideological implications were made radically explicit. In contrast with his City of the Captive Globe, the project that was meant to be the blueprint for this book, the examples are not a collection of eclectic modern "souvenirs" optimized by the grid, but a reasoned composition of radically different buildings that elucidates in miniature the logic of Manhattan.

One of Koolhaas's obsessions in New York City was the Waldorf-Astoria Hotel, which housed such a variety of services that the building itself was a veritable city.[40] Koolhaas's fixation with the typology of the metropolitan hotel—to which OMA devoted its early projects—resembled Ungers's focus on metropolitan superblocks like those he proposed for Tiergarten Viertel. For example, the superblock made of six towers placed atop a gigantic plinth, for which Koolhaas sketched an early proposal, was later recast in OMA's proposal for Welfare Island. In both cases, the metropolitan hotel becomes an assembly of programs and functions, to the point that the buildings themselves no longer have a specific program or function. Both Ungers's and OMA's projects were organized as two-part buildings: a plinth that contains public facilities and organizes access to the subway and trains, with towers for apartments and hotel rooms on top of the plinth. This composition was also tested in several projects done by Ungers's students (for example, Wolf Meyer-Christian's proposal for a multifunctional housing slab on Kaiserdamm, done in 1966), and has a precedent in the concept of the Hochhausstadt (vertical city) elaborated by Ludwig Hilberseimer in 1924. In his

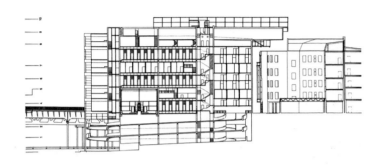

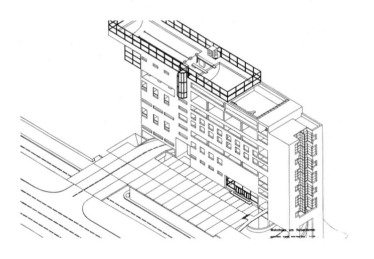

5.12
Wolf Meyer-Christian, student project for an apartment
building in Kaiserdamm, Berlin, 1966 (from O. M.
Ungers, *Schnellstrasse und Gebäude*, Berlin, 1966).

"ideal" project for a capitalist *Groszstadt*, Hilberseimer proposed to superimpose the main functions of the city within mixed-use city blocks rather than separating them in different zones of the city. The result was a city made by endlessly repeating a single building type consisting of vertically stacked programs. Hilberseimer's proposal, with hotel rooms as the main metropolitan living cell and a grid of transportation systems, accommodated the main driver of the capitalist metropolis: the mobility of workers. For Hilberseimer, mobility was more than a functional problem: it also embodied the radical process of social and cultural uprooting that created anonymous and generic space. Consequently, the architecture of the Hochhausstadt was a generic form made by the endless repetition of the same elements.

A similar formal and programmatic vocabulary is present in many of Ungers's own projects and in those done by his students in Berlin, including the proposals presented in his 1968 course, "Berlin 1995."[41] Yet for Ungers, and later for OMA, the concept of the "vertical city" was conveyed not by the horizontally extensive and repeatable system of Hilberseimer's Hochhausstadt, but rather by islands of intensity—collective forms of living—that pierced the endlessness of the individualized metropolis. The tension between the uprooting forces of the metropolis and an architecture that accommodates these forces characterizes both Ungers's and early OMA urban design. This theme is expressed in two OMA projects that, while they can be interpreted as an outgrowth of Ungers's architecture, are the starting point of Koolhaas and Zenghelis's "metropolitan architecture": Zenghelis's Hotel Sphinx (1975) and Koolhaas's Welfare Palace Hotel (1976).[42]

Both of these projects developed the typology of the hotel as the ultimate carrier of "cityness" within the agonized urbanity of 1970s New York. In both cases the building consists of a two-part composition: a base containing collective facilities, and towers

5.13
Elia Zenghelis, Hotel Sphinx in Times Square,
New York, 1975, axonometric view (painting by
Zoe Zenghelis). The hotel block as the ideal form
for social housing.

5.14
Rem Koolhaas, Welfare Palace Hotel, Roosevelt Island,
New York, 1976, cutaway axonometric (painting
by Madelon Vriesendorp). Architecture as the life raft
of the (decaying) city.

containing hotel rooms and more private shared facilities. For OMA, this composition was meant to replicate, at a "miniature" scale, the form of New York City with its repetition of towers and their endless fenestration. Following Ungers's method, in which the most controversial aspects of a site are idealized as the main drivers for a project, both the Hotel Sphinx, a social housing project proposed for the then-derelict Times Square, and the Welfare Palace Hotel, a social housing hotel proposed within a larger competition entry for the renewal of Welfare Island (now called Roosevelt Island), addressed New York's period of crisis by exaggerating and compressing into finite architectural projects the two faces of the capitalist city: extreme individual anonymity and a seemingly limitless potential for encounter.

Following in Ungers's steps, these two projects embraced the city even in its most wild and dangerous manifestations. Reacting against Rowe's skepticism toward modernist urban design, the OMA projects, like Ungers's Tiergarten Viertel and Lichterfelde, took on the modernist project's optimism at the prospect of designing the city, yet departed from modernism's comprehensive planning to propose a strategic retreat into a composition of finite, limited forms. The artifacts that dominate the derelict landscapes of the Tiergarten Viertel, Times Square, and Welfare Island predate Koolhaas's summary of this approach, which is contained in his most important theoretical manifesto, "Bigness" (1994).[43]

In "Bigness," Koolhaas makes explicit the principles that were embryonic in the earlier OMA projects. The architecture of bigness artificially reconstructs the city just as the city is under the assault of urbanization. "Bigness" refers to the scale of gigantic architectural forms—not those that develop horizontally, as in the case of megastructures or suburban sprawl, the two primary options for the American postwar city, but rather those that develop vertically as finite architectural forms. Due to their massive scale, these forms cannot be controlled by a single architect. For this reason, the architecture of bigness, as Ungers's work and OMA's early forms demonstrated, could only be anonymous simple forms, the scale of which schematizes authorship to the most generic architectural components. Here, authorless architecture is not simply the effect of scale and quantity; it is also the prerequisite for an architecture that is finite in its envelope, yet that allows maximum flexibility and indeterminacy in its interior.

Ungers anticipated this position in "Planning Criteria," a short text he published in 1976. He affirmed that a fundamental aspect of buildings that aspire to be "cities within the city" is their disposable form vis-à-vis further development and change, and that such a possibility is more feasible with a finite form, which, by being straightforward in its function, allows for its appropriation by the inhabitants.[44]

The most powerful representation of a city landscape produced by such an approach is an axonometric view of New York that includes Koolhaas's Welfare Island project. The proposal for Welfare Island (1975–1976) is rendered together with other Manhattan examples of "cities within the city" whose stories are narrated in *Delirious New York*: the RCA Building, the Hotel Sphinx, and the United Nations. These are depicted as islands in a tabula rasa Manhattan reduced to an empty grid. The Manhattan grid is also replicated on Welfare Island to create eight new blocks on the small island, in a way making it a miniature version of Manhattan. Ungers would apply the same strategy in his entry for the Roosevelt Island competition one year later, but with a difference: whereas OMA replicated a fragment of the grid at the same size as the original, Ungers introduced a miniature version of Central Park, which required him to reduce the size of the Manhattan blocks on the small island. Koolhaas conceived the grid as delineating "parking lots" for formally, programmatically, and ideologically competing architectures that would essentially confront one another from their identical "parking spaces."[45] His proposal, however, fills only four blocks. These blocks are a colossal "roadblock" straddling the Queensboro Bridge and containing a convention center, sport and entertainment facilities, and office space; a Kazimir Malevich suprematist Architecton (an architecture without program "to be conquered programmatically by a future civilization that deserves it"); a harbor carved out of rock that receives floating structures such as Norman Bel Geddes's "special streamlined yacht"; a park with a Chinese swimming pool; and at the tip of the island, the Welfare Palace Hotel.[46] The blocks are connected by a "travelator" that organizes the island in a linear sequence of different parts and then continues over the water to a "counter U-N building" sited across the river from the original in Manhattan. The composition is reminiscent of Exodus, and its logic can be traced back to Ungers's Grünzug Süd. In this case, it can be interpreted as a reading of a New York no longer seen as constituted by endless rows of skyscrapers but envisioned as a dialectical city of contrasting singular forms. Welfare Island becomes a sort of idealized version of Manhattan.

OMA's Welfare Island can be considered a radical development of Ungers's dialectical approach and an anti-*Collage City* project. As such, it radicalized the formal logic already present in Ungers's projects and anticipated Berlin as a Green Archipelago. Welfare Island's archipelago-like composition of exemplary architectures reconstructs the ideal integrity of the city, not as totalizing and pervasive urbanization nor as a conglomerate of fragments, but as a dialectical field made up of forces such as separation and contrast. For both Ungers and OMA, the potential of the city is generated by its most critical urban forces.

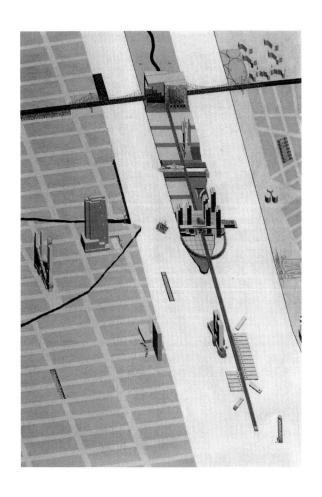

5.15
Rem Koolhaas, New Welfare Island,
Roosevelt Island, New York, 1976,
axonometric view facing Manhattan.

In the OMA project, as in Ungers's Tiergarten Viertel, the illusion of an architectural project that "improves" the city is replaced by an architecture that reifies in the most radical way the splintering forces of the metropolis that might otherwise remain ungraspable. From this perspective, Welfare Island can be interpreted as an extreme consequence of a scenario of decline in which New York—once the paradigm of congestion and density—survives a radical process of depopulation. Beyond being simply examples of New York's culture of congestion, the artifacts floating within the empty grid are also the last bastions of "cityness" left in this scenario of urban decadence. Architecture is thus projected as an *island*, the last opportunity for the city to become something and survive its decline.

The starting point for Berlin as a Green Archipelago was the urban crisis of Berlin in the 1970s. If urbanization fundamentally implies the capacity of the city to expand, to accommodate and even to trigger growth (both economic and demographic), one of the most crucial manifestations of urban crisis is the process of a city's depopulation. Depopulation has an immediate impact on the economy of a city because it undermines an essential factor of the urban economy: profit from land speculation. Moreover, the decreasing number of inhabitants in a city is connected with a fundamental problem of the social and economic management of cities: the idea of population as the link between demography, economy, and governance.[47] Since the seventeenth century, population has been the deus ex machina of the power politics that govern the city and the state, and depopulation has been considered the unequivocal sign of "bad" government.[48] As discussed in the first chapter, the discipline of urbanism is quintessentially linked with the maintenance of population; urbanization can be considered the material and organizational embodiment of the principle of population. In the history of population theories, urban growth has been the fundamental goal of government. For this reason, the possibility of growth has historically been the mission of any modernizing city project. Berlin as a Green Archipelago is the first project to break with this tradition and propose an opposite goal: the "undesirable" scenario of city *depopulation*.

Berlin as a Green Archipelago was based on the prediction, made at the end of the 1970s, that the next decade would see West Berlin's population drop dramatically.[49] What was unique in this scenario, even apocalyptic, was the city's status as a closed island within a hostile territory, making any flight to the suburbs impossible. Following his criteria of urban design, Ungers and his collaborators considered the crisis of a declining population not as a problem to solve but rather as the very engine of the project. This mechanism consisted in the reduction of the city's size to concentrated points, or city islands. As its main thesis, Berlin as a Green Archipelago promoted the demolition of zones of the city that had been abandoned or that were in a state of unstoppable decline, so that the project could focus only on the few selected parts of the city where residents were staying. Finally liberated from the impasse of urbanity, these parts of the city, in the form of islands, would compose a green archipelago in a natural "lagoon." The islands were conceived not as ex novo settlements but as a restructuring of existing situations. Following the strategy of Lichterfelde, Ungers proposed to insert typologies such as urban villas in order to densify these islands without filling the incomplete perimeter blocks of the city.

The selection of these "island zones" of the city was critical. Rather than being based on economic criteria, this selection was based on the possibility of discerning what had developed over time as cornerstones of the symbolic geography of the city. Another criterion for selection was the possibility of a dialectical complementarity between the selected parts of the city; each part that was chosen would be formally antithetical to one or two other parts. This criterion is fundamental to the logic of the archipelago, because it avoids the simple and ad hoc incremental addition of parts that is typical of urban sprawl. Accordingly, Ungers proposed to save and consolidate the southern part of Friedrichstadt Süd, Gorlitz station, the area around Schlosstrasse, and twentieth-century districts such as Märkisches Viertel, Gropiusstadt, and Onkel Toms Hütte, among other areas. These settlements were characteristically the products of precise ideological intentions about living and the city; thus each part was the embodiment of an idea of the city different from the others.

In order to heighten the distinctions of each form, Ungers associated each part with other city project paradigms, such as Friedrich Weinbrenner's plan for Karlsruhe, the Manhattan grid, or Leonidov's plan for the linear city of Magnitogorsk, using plans that were proposed for entire cities as paradigms for parts of the city. This process of association provided a nondeterministic means for the formal definition of city parts. Form in this case was not the imposition of one particular figure or image onto each of these city parts; here, form was understood as the possibility of association between existing situations and city paradigms. Thus, city form is not one particular image of the city but the possibility of forming moments within the city on the basis of architectural examples. In order to explain this strategy, Ungers referred to Schinkel's and Lenné's works at the Havellandschaft.[50] For Ungers, the approach of this particular project—a monumental complex developed as a territorial archipelago of radically different artifacts merged with the landscape of the Havel River—provided the most powerful paradigm through which to conceptualize Berlin itself as an archipelago city. Such an association between a monumental complex and a city avoids literal quotation of the reference and uses it only as a conceptual device through which to heighten the idea of existing situations and extract from them their latent form. Unlike Rowe's *Collage City*, where examples from the past are quoted literally, the system of associations presented by Ungers was meant to provide a field of references through which the architecture of the islands could be identified.

Another important aspect of the project was the "sea" in between the islands. While the islands were to be consolidated and eventually densified, the areas between the islands were to be left to the "informal" metabolism of a vast green area. These areas were imagined as forests, agricultural fields, gardens, and space for any sort of self-organized activity of the islands' inhabitants or of those who chose to live in this more informal and temporary habitat. In this sense, the "green" between the islands serves as an antithesis to the "cityness" of the islands. While the islands were imagined as the city, the area in between was intended to be the opposite: a world in which any idea or form of the city was deliberately left to its dissolution. In other words, the dialectical logic of the project implied that the more the islands were meant to heighten the logic of the city, the more the "sea" was supposed to "develop" as a mix of opposing tendencies: self-management, extreme suburbanization, and dark forest.

Ungers provided two opposing references for these green areas: on the one hand, the practice of what today would be called "zero-mile" agriculture—fields in which the inhabitants of the islands could manage their own food supply and thus make the economy of their settlement independent from larger systems; and on the other, the urban studies that Hilberseimer developed in Chicago between the 1940s and 1950s, in which he proposed to radically decentralize the city in the form of settlements immersed in a green landscape and served by motorways. This twofold, contradictory explanation for the "green" sea of the archipelago provoked the imagination and challenged assumptions about ecological urbanism, then on the rise, by showing how the notion of "green" could host such opposing scenarios as collective self-organization and absolute individualism. Ungers identified "green," or the void, as something permanently ambiguous that accommodates both extreme scenarios: withdrawn from urbanity and equally embracing it. These references created an opposition between the island and the sea as a dialog between something with intelligible borders and something unstable and in permanent flux. Moreover, the limit, or "shoreline," between the sea and the islands was crucial. In this way, the project implied that the more the form of certain city parts was clearly defined, the more other parts would be released from definition, and vice versa. This idea was rehearsed and radicalized by Koolhaas in his 1985 text "Imagining Nothingness," where he proposed to think the project of the city by starting from what Berlin as a Green Archipelago indicated as the green sea.[51]

Ungers's architectural islands in Berlin as a Green Archipelago can be considered both as self-referential entities and as city parts that, through their position and insular form, frame what escapes legibility: the inescapable sea of urbanization. In this way, architectural form becomes the index of its opposite: that which escapes the stability of architecture. Berlin as a Green Archipelago postulates a city form that, in order to be defined, requires confrontation with its opposite—urbanization—and with the city's most controversial aspects, such as division, conflict, and even destruction. At the same time, such an idea of the city postulates a form in which even the most disruptive forces can be framed by the possibility of giving them a form—that is, the possibility of establishing criteria of knowledge and reification of these disruptive forces in the form of architectural examples. *The city within the city* is thus not only the literal staging of the city's lost form within the limits of architectural artifacts; it is also, and especially, the possibility of considering architectural form as a *point of entry* toward the project of the city. In this sense, architecture is not only a physical object; architecture is also what survives the idea of the city.

NOTES

INTRODUCTION

1. For an analysis of the idea of the absolute, see Giorgio Agamben, "*Se*: Hegel's Absolute and Heidegger's *Ereignis*," in *Potentialities: Collected Essays in Philosophy*, ed. and trans. Daniel Holler-Roazen (Stanford: Stanford University Press, 1999), 116–137.

CHAPTER 1

1. See Scott Meikle, *Aristotle's Economic Thought* (Oxford: Clarendon Press, 1995).
2. Initially the Greek term *polis* indicated a fortress. Later the term was used to name a community organized in the form of a state. The Greek *polis* is always a city-state. See Paolo Morachiello, *La città greca* (Bari: Laterza, 2003), 51.
3. For example, Virgil says in the *Aeneid* that "Aeneas designates the city with the plow" (*Aeneas urbem designat aratro*). On the difference between the *polis* and the *civitas*, see Massimo Cacciari, *La città* (Pazzini: Verrucchio, 2004). For the etymological roots of the words *urbs* and *civitas*, see Luigi Castiglioni and Scevola Margotti, *Vocabolario della lingua latina* (Turin: Loescher, 1966).
4. Hannah Arendt, "Introduction into Politics," in Arendt, *The Promise of Politics*, ed. Jerome Kohn (New York: Schocken Books, 2005), 186–187. On the concept of *nomos*, see also Carl Schmitt, *The Nomos of the Earth in the International Law of the Jus Publicum Europaeum*, trans. G. L. Ulmen (London: Telos Press, 1974). For an interpretation of the concept of *nomos* and its crisis, see Massimo Cacciari, *Geofilosofia dell'Europa* (Milan: Adelphi, 2003). Originally used to mean "pasture," *nomos* came to mean "the partition of land" (*nèmein*). For the ancient Greeks the fundamental law was the configuration and partition of land according to this original way of settlement.
5. "To the Greek mind," writes Arendt, "this lack of moderation [insatiability] did not lie in the immoderateness of the man who acts, or in his hubris, but in the fact that the relationships arising through action are and must be of the sort that keep extending without limits. By linking men of action together, each relationship

established by action ends up in a web of ties and relationships in which it triggers new links, changes the constellation of existing relationships, and thus always reaches out ever further, setting much more into interconnected motion than the man who initiates action ever could have foreseen. The Greeks countered this thrust toward limitlessness with the *nomos*, limiting action to what happens between men within a polis and when, as inevitably happened, action drew the polis into matters lying beyond it, such matters were referred back to the polis." Arendt, "Introduction into Politics," 186–187.

6. Ibid, 187.
7. Ibid., 185.
8. On the archipelago as geopolitical form, see Massimo Cacciari, *L'arcipelago* (Milan: Adelphi, 1997).
9. This fundamental difference can be fully understood in the way the Greeks and the Romans would create colonies. For the Greeks, colonies that were trade centers were largely politically independent, while colonies that were founded by people who had escaped from other *poleis* for political reasons were often fully independent. In other words, a colony was largely autonomous from the "mother city" (in ancient Greek, *metropolis*), from which the "colonizers" originally came, meaning an existing *polis* could replicate itself but not expand its domain. For the Romans, the colonies were simply territories annexed to the power of Rome, and thus were included in the totality of the empire.
10. It is interesting to see how Cerdà went through a painstaking philological (and philosophical) process to decouple the words *urbs* and *civitas* in order to make the former the center of theory, as he intended his concept of urbanization to go beyond the traditional frame of the city. See Ildefons Cerdà, *The Five Bases of the General Theory of Urbanization*, ed. Arturo Soria y Puig, trans. Bernard Miller and Mary Fons i Fleming (Madrid: Electa España, 1999), 81. This book is a partial translation of Cerdà's *Teoría general de la urbanización* (Madrid, 1867).
11. *Cives* comes from *civis*, "citizen," and ultimately from an Indo-European root that means "to settle." See Manlio Cortellazzo and Paolo Zolli, *Dizionario etimologico della lingua italiana* (Bologna: Zanichelli, 1979), s.v. "Cives."
12. For an accurate description of this process, see Paul M. Hohenberg and Lynn Hollen Lees, *The Making of Urban Europe, 1000–1994* (Cambridge, MA: Harvard University Press, 1995).

13. On this fundamental paradox of modern Western civilization, see the reflections of Jürgen Habermas in *The Structural Transformation of the Public Sphere: An Inquiry into a Category of Bourgeois Society*, trans. Thomas Burger (Cambridge, MA: MIT Press, 1989).

14. See S. Lyman Tyler, "Spanish Laws Concerning Discoveries, Pacifications, and Settlements among the Indians, with an Introduction and the First English Translation of the *New Ordinances of Philip II, July 1573*, and of Book IV from the *Recopilacion de Leyes de las Indias* Relating to These Subjects" (Occasional Paper, no. 18, American West Center, College of Humanities, University of Utah, Salt Lake City, 1980).

15. In his commentary to the English translation of Cerdà's *Teoría general de la urbanización*, Arturo Soria y Puig remarks that the most important books or treatises on urbanism between the nineteenth century and the beginning of the twentieth never mention the now common word *urbanization* or its derivatives *urban* and *urbanity*. *Urbanisme* appeared in French in 1842, but it failed to become a common word until later. See Cerdà, *The Five Bases of the General Theory of Urbanization*, 79.

16. Conscious of how language itself is the primary material both of theory and of practice, Cerdà introduces the invention of the word *urbanization*: "Before launching into the study of the subject [the theory of urbanization], it is advisable … to start with definitions and explanations of the most usual words within that subject. …With all the more reasons than any other author, I find myself obliged to follow this rational custom, I who am going to lead the reader to the study of a new subject, a completely new, intact, virgin one, in which everything being new, even the words, which I had to seek and invent, had to be new, since, as I need to broadcast my new ideas, I was unable to find expressions for them in any panlexicon. Faced with the dilemma of either inventing a word or failing to write about a subject which I had come to believe ever more useful to society the deeper I have delved into studying it, I preferred to invent and write rather than to remain silent." Cerdà, *The Five Bases of the General Theory of Urbanization*, 79–80.

17. Ibid., 79.

18. Precisely to avoid the concept of the city as the locus of citizenship, and thus as a political form, Cerdà returned to the concept of *urbs*. In describing Cerdà's painstaking process of selecting the best term to describe the object of his theory, Soria y Puig writes: "The term that Cerdà initially thought of to designate the subject

of the new theory was *ciudad* (city), which is what he used in his first writings on urban planning and in the title of his first book with some theoretical ambition, the 1859 *Theory of City Building*. But the word *city*, as he explained some years later, did not totally satisfy him since it was an amphibological term, particularly in mind of its Latin origin *civitas*" (ibid., 79, 83, 80).

19. The word *suburbio* existed before Cerdà invented *urbanización*. As Soria y Puig remarks, Cerdà first used the derivatives of the word *urbs*, such as *suburbio*, in order to find a more suitable word for an unspecified group of dwellings, which led him to the word's root, *urbs* (ibid., 83).

20. Ibid., 87.

21. As is well known, the original layout of Cerdà's project was largely compromised by the densification of the blocks. However, the evolution of the city benefited immensely from the rational planning of the infrastructure. On the history and process of the realization of Cerdà's Barcelona, see Joan Busquets with the Harvard University Graduate School of Design, *Barcelona: The Urban Evolution of a Compact City* (Rovereto: Nicolodi; Cambridge, MA: Harvard University Graduate School of Design, 2005).

22. Ibid., 31.

23. This particular Foucauldian reading of Cerdà has been made by Andrea Cavalletti in his studies on the relationship between the foundation of urbanism as discipline and the rise of biopolitics as a method of governance during the eighteenth and nineteenth centuries. According to Cavalletti, who conducted his studies under the supervision of Giorgio Agamben, Cerdà's *General Theory* played an important role in establishing the paradigm of biopolitical administration of the territory in the discipline of making cities. Andrea Cavalletti, *La città biopolitica: Mitologie della sicurezza* (Milan: Bruno Mondadori, 2005), 20–32.

24. As a socialist and reformer, Cerdà thought that industrialization sometimes had bad consequences, but was not at all bad in its causes and principles. Thus his work must be understood as an attempt to solve the contradictions between industrialization and (capitalist) accumulation by upgrading the condition of the working class. However, it is precisely in this attempt that it is possible to see the subtle dialectic that always exists between the social upgrading of the workers and their political repression. My reading of the social upgrading of the working class as the supreme form of its political repression, which I also apply to my

interpretation of Cerdà's work, has been largely influenced by Operaist theories about the organization of the labor force and its transformation into work. See Raniero Panzieri, "Sull'uso delle macchine nel neocapitalismo," *Quaderni Rossi* 1 (1961): 53–72.

25. See Françoise Choay, *L'urbanisme, utopies et réalités: Une anthologie* (Paris: Éditions du Seuil, 1965).

26. Giorgio Agamben, *Il Regno e la Gloria: Per una genealogia teologica dell'economia e del governo* (Vicenza: Neri Pozza, 2007), 31.

27. Ludwig Hilberseimer, *Groszstadt Architektur* (Stuttgart: Julius Hoffmann Verlag, 1927).

28. Le Corbusier, "Une ville contemporaine," in *Oeuvre complète, 1910–1929*, ed. Willy Boesiger and Oscar Stonorov (Zurich: Éditions d'Architecture, 1964), 34–43. Gabriele Mastrigli has proposed a close reading of the "classical" figures that can be identified in Le Corbusier's Contemporary City for Three Million Inhabitants. See Gabriele Mastrigli, "In Praise of Discontinuity," in Christine de Baan, Joachim Declerck, Veronique Patteeuw, and the Berlage Instituut, *Visionary Power: Producing the Contemporary City* (Rotterdam: NAi Publishers, 2007), 113–124.

29. See Hannah Arendt, *The Human Condition* (Chicago: University of Chicago Press, 1958).

30. As Lee argues, "the Sixties are endless in staging endlessness as cultural phenomenon. Of revealing, in the long shadows cast by its technological entropy, a vision of the future ever quickening and repeating. This is one legacy of sixties art that continues to haunt us today." Pamela M. Lee, *Chronophobia: On Time in the Art of the 1960s* (Cambridge, MA: MIT Press, 2004), 259.

31. Georg Wilhelm Friedrich Hegel, *The Encyclopaedia Logic*, trans. T. F. Geraets, W. A. Suchting, and H. S. Harris (Indianapolis: Hackett, 1991), 149.

32. The theses concerning what Archizoom later called No-Stop City were presented in 1970 in the pages of *Casabella* with the significant title "Città, catena di montaggio del sociale" (City, assembly line of the social). The project was first published in 1971 as "No-Stop City: Residential Parkings, Climatic Universal System," in the magazine *Domus*. See Archizoom Associati, "Città, catena di montaggio del sociale: Ideologia e teoria della metropoli," *Casabella*, no. 350–351 (1970); Archizoom Associati, "No-Stop City: Residential Parkings, Climatic Universal System," *Domus*, no. 496 (1971). For a detailed description of the project, see Andrea

Branzi, *No-Stop City: Archizoom Associati* (Orleáns: Éditions HYX, 2006), which contains English translations of the magazine texts.

33. Archizoom members Massimo Morozzi and Gilberto Corretti often took part in the gatherings of the Operaisti, both in Turin at the time of Raniero Panzieri's journal *Quaderni Rossi* (1962–1964), and in Florence at the time of Mario Tronti's journal *Classe Operaia* (1964–1966). I have reconstructed the intense relationship between Archizoom and Operaismo in *The Project of Autonomy: Politics and Poetics within and against Capitalism* (New York: Princeton Architectural Press, 2008).

34. Mario Tronti, *Operai e capitale* (Turin: Einaudi, 1966), 66.

35. Ibid., 262.

36. As the members of Archizoom argued, this ultimate clash could have been possible if the political debate over the city had shifted from the problem of changing and reforming the existing city to the question of taking power over it by making clear its real mechanisms of control and reproduction. See Branzi, *No-Stop City: Archizoom Associati*, 162–163.

37. Ibid., 142.

38. The project consists of one panel and was first published in 1977 in a monographic issue of *Architectural Design* devoted to OMA; in 1978 it was reprinted in the appendix of *Delirious New York* (New York: Oxford University Press, 1978). For a more recent edition, see Rem Koolhaas, *Delirious New York: A Retroactive Manifesto for Manhattan* (New York: Monacelli Press, 1994), 294–296; subsequent references to this text are to this edition.

39. Ibid., 296.

40. Ibid.

41. Ibid.

42. Rem Koolhaas and the Harvard Graduate School of Design Project on the City, *Great Leap Forward* (Cologne: Taschen, 2001), 26.

43. See Oswald Mathias Ungers and Stefan Vieths, *The Dialectic City* (Milan: Skira, 1997).

44. Arendt, "Introduction into Politics," 93.

45. Ibid., 95.

46. See Carl Schmitt, *The Concept of the Political* (Chicago: University of Chicago Press, 1996). My combination of Arendt's definition of politics as the space of plurality and Schmitt's controversial concept of the political as the dual friend/enemy distinction is deliberately provocative. I believe that while Schmitt's concept suffers

from the political context in which it was theorized by the German jurist, Arendt's definition may suffer from the political correctness in which the idea of plurality has come to be used today. Thus I propose the following possible formula: Arendt + Schmitt. In other words, as it is no longer possible to read Schmitt's belligerent concept without Arendt's much broader conception of political life, it is also not possible to read Arendt's optimism toward individual responsibility without Schmitt's political realism.

47. In the most fundamental passage of *The Concept of the Political*, Schmitt emphasizes that the possibility of the autonomy of the political is not self-referential despotism, but rather a profound relational condition: "Thereby the inherently objective nature and autonomy of the political becomes evident by virtue of its being able to treat, distinguish, and comprehend the friend-enemy antithesis independently of other antitheses." Ibid., 27.

48. See Carl Schmitt, "Total Enemy, Total War," in *Four Articles, 1931–1938*, trans. Simona Draghici (Washington, DC: Plutarch Press, 1999), 23.

49. *Inimicus* is the "personal" enemy, stemming from a feeling of personal antipathy. *Hostis* is the "public" enemy, the enemy that challenges a collective group of individuals. Thus the concept of enemy as *hostis*, in spite of its immediate meaning, is a fundamental category that addresses the idea of publicness and collectivity. As Schmitt writes: "The enemy is not merely a competitor or just any partner of a conflict in general. He is also not the private adversary whom one hates. An enemy exists only when, at least potentially, one fighting collectivity of people confronts a similar collectivity." See Schmitt, *The Concept of the Political*, 28–29.

50. Heinrich Meier, *The Lesson of Carl Schmitt: Four Chapters on the Distinction between Political Theology and Political Philosophy*, trans. Marcus Brainard (Chicago: University of Chicago Press, 1998), 76.

51. Arendt, "Introduction into Politics," 99.

52. This antithesis should not be understood "visually" as a figure-ground relationship, but in a much broader, conceptual and existential sense. Eventually figure-ground can be one possibility of this distinction, but it is not at all the only one (and not even the most interesting).

53. See Jeanne Hersch, *L'être et la forme* (Neuchâtel: Éditions de la Baconnière, 1946), 68.

54. Ibid., 73.

55. These propositions were discussed in part with Joan Ockman as points of de-
    parture of the For(u)m, a two-year program exploring the relationships between
    politics and contemporary life. The For(u)m project was organized under the
    auspices of the Temple Hoyne Buell Center for the Development of American
    Architecture at the Graduate School of Architecture, Planning, and Preservation,
    Columbia University, during the academic years 2006–2007 and 2007–2008.

56. See, for example, the work and ideas of the movement called "new urbanism,"
    which is one of the most extreme manifestations of the ethos of urbanization in
    terms of economic segregation.

57. See Rem Koolhaas, Stefano Boeri, Sanford Kwinter, Nadia Tazi, Hans Ulrich
    Obrist, et al., *Mutations* (Barcelona: Actar, 2001); Arjen Mulder et al., *TransUrbanism*
    (Rotterdam: NAi Publishers/V2_Publishing, 2002); Edward Soja, *Postmetropolis:
    Critical Studies of Cities and Regions* (Oxford: Blackwell, 2000); Rita Schneider-
    Silwa, *City on the Move: Globalization, Political Change, and Urban Development*
    (Vienna: Hatje Cantz, 1999); *Cities in Transition* (Dordrecht: Springer, 2006).

58. See Werner Oechslin, "'Not from an Aestheticizing, but from a General Point of
    View': Mies's Steady Resistance to Formalism and Determinism: A Plea for Value-
    Criteria in Architecture," in Phyllis Lambert, ed., *Mies in America* (New York:
    Whitney Museum of American Art and Harry N. Abrams, 2001), 22–89.

59. Manfredo Tafuri and Francesco Dal Co, *Architettura contemporanea* (Milan: Electa,
    1976), 301–309; trans. Robert Erich Wolf as *Modern Architecture* (New York: Harry
    N. Abrams, 1979).

60. Albert Pope, *Ladders* (New York: Princeton Architectural Press, 1996).

61. To quote the title of an important study that Hilberseimer made on the project of
    the American city. See Ludwig Hilberseimer, *The New Regional Pattern: Industries
    and Gardens, Workshops and Farms* (Chicago: Paul Theobald, 1949).

62. See Manfredo Tafuri, *Progetto e utopia: Architettura e sviluppo capitalistico* (Bari:
    Laterza, 1973), 64.

63. See Sven-Olov Wallenstein, *The Silences of Mies* (Stockholm: AXL Books, 2008).

64. See Tafuri, *Progetto e utopia*; Tafuri and Dal Co, *Modern Architecture*; Massimo Cac-
    ciari, *Architecture and Nihilism: On the Philosophy of Modern Architecture*, trans.
    Stephen Sartarelli (New Haven: Yale University Press, 1993); K. Michael Hays,
    "Critical Architecture: Between Culture and Norm," *Perspecta* 21 (1984); Detlef
    Mertins, "Mies's Skyscraper 'Project': Towards the Redemption of Techni-

cal Structure," in Detlef Mertins, ed., *The Presence of Mies* (New York: Princeton Architectural Press, 1994), 49–67. The quotation is from Wallenstein, *The Silences of Mies*, 91.

65. Fritz Neumeyer, "Space for Reflection: Block versus Pavillion," in Franz Schulze, ed., *Mies van der Rohe: Critical Essays* (New York: Museum of Modern Art, 1989), 148–171.

66. Oswald Mathias Ungers, "Mies van der Rohe and Toronto," *Lotus* 112 (March 2002): 108–131. Ungers reads Mies's use of the plinth in his North American complexes, such as the Toronto-Dominion Centre, as an attempt to design a city form from within the limited boundaries of the architectural artifact. Addressed in this way, the plinth becomes the element that transforms the limits of the architectural artifact into its fundamental contribution to the city form.

67. Cacciari, *L'arcipelago*, 20–21.

CHAPTER 2

1. Rudolf Wittkower, "Principles of Palladio's Architecture," parts 1 and 2, *Journal of the Warburg and Courtauld Institutes*, no. 7 (1944): 102–122; no. 8 (1944): 68–102. Reprinted in Rudolf Wittkower, *Architectural Principles in the Age of Humanism* (London: Warburg Institute, 1949).

2. Colin Rowe, "The Mathematics of the Ideal Villa: Palladio and Le Corbusier Compared," *Architectural Review* (May 1950): 289–300.

3. James S. Ackerman, *The Villa: Form and Ideology of Country Houses* (Princeton: Princeton University Press, 1990), 10–14.

4. The name Palladio comes from *Pallade*, a nickname given to Pallas Athena. In Greek, *pallax* means "young" and the *Palladium* was a wood statue of Pallas Athena. It became a famous image of ancient Greco-Roman mythology and was believed to keep a city safe. The name was probably chosen by Trissino in reference to Angel Palladio, a character in his poem *Italia liberata dai Goti*. Trissino's choice of this name makes explicit the cultural intentions he saw embodied in the young architect—in Trissino's militant (and slightly delirious) classicism, Palladio was the resurrection of an ancient architect. On the sources of Palladio's name, see Franco Barbieri, ed., *Architetture palladiane* (Vicenza: Neri Pozza, 1992), 211–212.

5. See Flavia Cantatore, "Casa Civena e i primi studi di Andrea Palladio per case e palazzi," in Franco Barbieri, ed., *Palladio 1508–2008: Il simposio del cinquecentenario* (Venice: Marsilio, 2008), 245–249.

6. Pierfilippo Castelli, *La vita di Giovangiorgio Trissino, oratore e poeta* (Venice: Giovanni Radici, 1753), 75. See also Franco Barbieri, "Giangiorgio Trissino e Andrea Palladio," in *Atti del convegno di studi su Giangiorgio Trissino* (Vicenza: Neri Pozza, 1980).

7. The same promotion of Roman architecture would be embraced by Daniele Barbaro, another patrician and diplomat, who supported Palladio after Trissino's death in 1550.

8. See Francesco Paolo di Teodoro, "Andrea Palladio e il lascito teorico di Raffaello: alcune osservazioni," in Barbieri, *Architetture palladiane*, 80–86.

9. See Peter Vaughan Hart and Peter Hicks, eds., *Palladio's Rome* (New Haven: Yale University Press, 2006).

10. Guido Beltramini, "Andrea Palladio 1508–1580," in Barbieri, *Palladio 1508–2008*, 2–4. See also Giangiorgio Zorzi, *Le opere pubbliche e i palazzi di Andrea Palladio* (Vicenza: Neri Pozza, 1965), 167–169.

11. For an overview of the urban and political history of Venice, see Franco Barbieri, *Vicenza: Storia di una avventura urbana* (Milano: Silvana Editoriale, 1982). See also Guido Beltramini, *Palladio privato* (Venice: Marsilio, 2008), 14.

12. Barbieri, *Vicenza*, 54, 68.

13. See Andrea Palladio, *The Four Books on Architecture*, trans. Robert Tavernor and Richard Schofield (Cambridge, MA: MIT Press, 1997), 82.

14. On the idea of the villa, see Ackerman, *The Villa: Form and Ideology of Country Houses*.

15. This one, infamous exception was Giuliano da Sangallo's Villa Medici at Poggio a Caiano (1485).

16. Stefano Ray, "Integrità e ambiguità," in Kurt Foster, ed., *Palladio: Ein Symposium* (Rome: Schweizerisches Institut in Rom, 1980), 53–74.

17. For an analysis of the link between Palladio's architecture and the reform of the Serenissima's Terraferma, see Denis Cosgrove, *The Palladian Landscape: Geographical Change and Its Cultural Representations in Sixteenth-Century Italy* (University Park: Pennsylvania State University Press, 1993).

18. See Gino Benzoni, ed., *Verso la Santa Agricoltura: Ruzzante, il Polesine* (Rovigo: Associazione Culturale Minelliana, 2004).

19. See Palladio, *The Four Books on Architecture*, 18–20.

20. On the Venetian projects of Sabbadino and Cornaro, see Manfredo Tafuri, *Venice and the Renaissance* (Cambridge, MA: MIT Press, 1995), 139–160.

21. Ibid., 146.

22. Ibid., 58.

23. Ibid.

24. On the elevation of the Greek *oikos* as a principle of city management, see Giorgio Agamben, *Il potere e la gloria* (Vicenza: Neri Pozza, 2007).

25. Palladio, *The Four Books on Architecture*, 149–150.

26. Giorgio Agamben, "Che cosa è un paradigma?" in Giorgio Agamben, *Signata rerum: Sul metodo* (Turin: Bollati Boringhieri, 2008), 20.

27. Paolo Virno, *Mondanità: L'idea di "mondo" tra esperienza sensibile e sfera pubblica* (Rome: Manifestolibri, 1994), 106.

28. On Palladio's war architecture, see Guido Beltramini, "Palladio e l'architettura della battaglia: Le edizioni illustrate di Cesare Polibio," in Barbieri, *Palladio 1508–2008*, 217–229.

CHAPTER 3

1. The link between Piranesi's *Antichità romane* and the tradition of *instauratio urbis* has been proposed by Lola Kantor-Kazovsky in her book *Piranesi as Interpreter of Roman Architecture and the Origins of His Intellectual World* (Florence: Leo S. Olschki Editore, 2006).

2. On the link between Piranesi's *Campo Marzio* and Bonaventura van Overbeke's plan of ancient Rome, see Marcello Fagiolo, "L'immagine di Roma," in Mario Bevilacqua, ed., *Nolli, Vasi e Piranesi: Immagine di Roma antica e moderna. Rappresentare e conoscere la metropolis dei Lumi* (Roma: Artemide, 2004), 37–48.

3. For a critical overview of these maps, see Margaret Scherer, *Marvels of Ancient Rome* (New York: Phaidon Press for the Metropolitan Museum of Art, 1955), 5–6.

4. Baldassarre Castiglione wrote a letter to the pope that was intended to introduce Raphael's drawings of ancient ruins in Rome. In this letter, Castiglione, interpreting Raphael's ideas, proposed for the first time the rigorous use of orthogonal projections in depicting ancient ruins in place of the pictorial convention of perspectival drawing. Several historians have read the letter as a clear project in which the preservation and maintenance of ancient ruins is directly linked with the urban development of the modern city. Raphael proposed the preservation

of ruins not as a mere act of historical piety but, following Bramante, as the cultivation of examples for the definition of new architectural models. See Gabriele Morolli, *"Le belle forme degli Antichi": Raffaello e il progetto del primo trattato rinascimentale sulle antichità di Roma* (Florence: Alinea, 1984).

5. For a detailed history of Ligorio's *Antiquae urbis imago*, see Howard Burns, "Pirro Ligorio's Reconstruction of Ancient Rome: The *Antiquae Urbis Imago* of 1561," in *Pirro Ligorio: Artist and Antiquarian* (Milan: Silvana Editoriale, 1988), 19–92.

6. Werner Oechslin, "L'intérêt archéologique et l'expérience architecturale avant et après Piranèse," in *Piranèse et les Français: Colloque tenu à la Villa Médicis, 12–14 mai 1976*, ed. Georges Brunel (Rome: Edizioni dell'Elefante, 1976), 395–410.

7. See Le Corbusier, *Toward an Architecture*, trans. John Goodman (Los Angeles: Getty Publications, 2007), 200.

8. On the relationship between Piranesi's *Campo Marzio*, Pirro Ligorio's *Imago*, and Le Corbusier's Lesson of Rome, see Gabriele Mastrigli, "In Praise of Discontinuity," in Christine de Baan, ed., *Power: Producing the Contemporary City* (Rotterdam: NAi Publishers, 2007), 45–54.

9. See Manfredo Tafuri, *Ricerca del Rinascimento: Principi, città, architetti* (Turin: Einaudi, 1992), 37–38.

10. Walter Ullmann, *A History of Political Thought: The Middle Ages* (Baltimore: Penguin Books, 1965), 106.

11. Tafuri, *Ricerca del Rinascimento*, 34.

12. For a comprehensive history of Nicholas V's plan for Rome and its cultural and political implications, see Franco Borsi, *Nicolò V e Roma: Alberti, Angelico, Manetti e un grande piano urbano* (Florence: Polistampa, 2009).

13. On the work of Poggio Bracciolini and Flavio Biondo and their interconnections, see Eugenio Garin, *Umanisti, artisti e scienziati: Studi sul Rinascimento italiano* (Rome: Editori Riuniti, 1989), 39–47.

14. See Arnald Bruschi, *Bramante*, trans. Peter Murray (London: Thames and Hudson, 1977).

15. See Brian A. Curran, Anthony Grafton, Pamela O. Long, and Benjamin Weiss, *Obelisk: A History* (Cambridge, MA: MIT Press, 2009), 103–140.

16. See Mary Sponberg Pedley, "Scienza e cartografia: Roma nell'epoca dei Lumi," in Bevilacqua, *Nolli, Vasi e Piranesi*, 37–48.

17. Ibid., 42.

18. For the most historically detailed account of the *Nuova pianta di Roma*, see Mario Bevilacqua, *Roma nel secolo dei Lumi: Architettura, erudizione, scienza nella pianta di Giovanni Battista Nolli "celebre geometra"* (Napoli: Electa Napoli, 1998).

19. Louis Marin, "The City in Its Map and Portrait," in *On Representation*, trans. Catherine Porter (Stanford: Stanford University Press, 2001), 202–218.

20. Mario Bevilacqua, "Nolli, Piranesi, e Vasi: Percorsi e incontri nella città del Settecento," in Bevilacqua, *Nolli, Vasi e Piranesi*, 23.

21. On the relationship between Nolli and Vasi, see Mario Gori Sassoli, "Sulle magnificenze di Roma antica e moderna di Giuseppe Vasi," in Mario Gori Sassoli and Giuseppe Vasi, *Magnificenza di Roma antica e moderna* (Roma: Salerno Editrice, 1992).

22. This is the argument advanced by Wittkower in his important essay on Piranesi. See Rudolf Wittkower, "Piranesi's Architectural Creed," in *Studies in the Italian Baroque* (Boulder: Westview Press, 1975).

23. See Kantor-Kazovsky, *Piranesi as Interpreter of Roman Architecture*, 144–156.

24. Ibid., 143–192.

25. Ibid., 134.

26. Mario Bevilacqua in *Nolli, Vasi e Piranesi*, 29.

27. Kantor-Kazovsky, *Piranesi as Interpreter of Roman Architecture*, 59–118.

CHAPTER 4

1. Aldo Rossi, introduction to Étienne-Louis Boullée, *Architettura, saggio sull'arte*, trans. Aldo Rossi (Padua: Marsilio, 1967), 4–14. The English edition is Étienne-Louis Boullée, "Architecture, Essay on Art," in *Boullée's Treatise on Architecture*, ed. Helen Rosenau (London: Alec Tiranti, 1953).

2. See Sylvia Lavin, *Quatremère de Quincy and the Invention of a Modern Language of Architecture* (Cambridge, Mass.: MIT Press, 1992).

3. Boullée devoted another treatise to the topic of residential architecture, but only its table of contents, written by Boullée himself, survives. Some of the projects of this treatise are known by copies made by his students such as Jean-Nicolas-Louis Durand and Antoine-Marie Peire. See Jean-Marie Pérouse de Montclos, *Étienne-Louis Boullée 1728–1799* (Milan: Electa, 1997), 160–164. However, Boullée described the topic of "private" architecture as "sterile."

4. Boullée, "Architecture, Essay on Art," 12.

5. See Pérouse de Montclos, *Étienne-Louis Boullée*, 139.

6. Aldo Rossi, *L'architettura della città* (Padua: Marsilio, 1966).

7. For a general discussion of the idea and history of French classicism, see Anthony Blunt and Richard Beresford, *Art and Architecture in France, 1500–1700* (New Haven: Yale University Press, 1999).

8. See Anthony Gerbino, "François Blondel, 1618–1686: Architecture, Erudition, and Early Modern Science" (PhD diss., Columbia University, 2002).

9. On Colbert's politics of state management, see Jacob Soll, *The Information Master: Jean-Baptiste Colbert's Secret State Intelligence System* (Ann Arbor: University of Michigan Press, 2009).

10. A fundamental study of the *hôtel* as an originator of the urbanity of Paris in modern times is Michael Dennis, *Court and Garden: From the French Hôtel to the City of Modern Architecture* (Cambridge, Mass.: MIT Press, 1986).

11. For an in-depth historical analysis of Place Royale, see Hilary Ballon, *The Paris of Henry IV: Architecture and Urbanism* (Cambridge, Mass.: MIT Press, 1991), 57–113.

12. Pierre Le Muet, *Manière de bastir pour touttes sortes de personnes* (Paris: Melchior Tavernier, 1623).

13. My discussion here is based on Carlo Olmo's reading of Pierre Patte's plan as a paradigm of the emergence of modern spatiality. See Carlo Maria Olmo, *Le nuvole di Patte: Quattro lezioni di storia urbana* (Milan: Franco Angeli, 1995), 55–73.

14. Antoine Picon, *French Architects and Engineers in the Age of Enlightenment*, trans. Martin Thom (Cambridge: Cambridge University Press, 1992), 107.

15. Michel Foucault, *Naissance de la biopolitique: Cours au Collège de France 1978–1979* (Paris: Gallimard, 2004).

16. Picon, *French Architects and Engineers in the Age of Enlightenment*, 113.

17. In this sense, it is interesting to note that Boullée himself was familiar with the engineers' metropolitan space, because he was actively collaborating with the preparatory work for the map of Paris executed by the engineer Gaspard de Prony, who was commissioned by the Revolutionary government to produce a cadastral map of France. See Pérouse de Montclos, *Étienne-Louis Boullée 1728–1799*, 69.

18. See Emil Kaufmann, *Three Revolutionary Architects: Ledoux, Boullée, Lequeu* (Philadelphia: American Philosophical Society, 1952).

19. Boullée, "Architecture, Essay on Art," 87.

20. Ibid., 101.

21. Rossi, introduction to Boullée, *Architettura, saggio sull'arte*, 12.

22.	See Carl Schmitt, *Political Theology: Four Chapters on the Concept of Political Sovereignty*, trans. George Schwab (Chicago: University of Chicago Press, 1995).

CHAPTER 5

1.	Oswald Mathias Ungers, Rem Koolhaas, Peter Riemann, Hans Kollhoff, Arthur Ovaska, Cities within the City: Proposal by the Sommer Akademie for Berlin. The model of the city in the city, or Berlin as a Green Archipelago, was organized on a general basis during Cornell University's Sommer Akademie in Berlin in 1977; it was designed by the senator in charge of building and housing systems and by the Künstlerhaus Bethanien. See Oswald Mathias Ungers et al., *Die Stadt in der Stadt: Berlin, das Grüne Stadtarchipel: Ein stadträumliches Planungskonzept für die zukünftige Entwicklung Berlins* (Berlin: Studioverlag für Architektur, 1977). For English and Italian translations of the project, see *Lotus* 19 (1978): 82–97.

2.	For an overview of Ungers's studios between 1964 and 1977, see *Arch+* 181/182 (2006).

3.	The German architect Josef Paul Kleihues, director of the Internationale Bauausstellung (IBA) from 1978 to 1984, was very much influenced by Leon and Rob Krier's conviction that the city needs streets, blocks, and squares. See Josef Paul Kleihues, "Stations in the Architectural History of Berlin in the 20th Century: IBA," *A+U Extra Edition on International Building Exhibition Berlin* (1987): 218–236.

4.	See Paul Stangl, "The Vernacular and the Monumental: Memory and Landscapes in Post-war Berlin," *Geojournal* 73, no. 3 (November 2008): 245–253.

5.	See Oswald Mathias Ungers, "Zum projekt Neue Stadt in Koln," *Werk* 50, no. 7 (July 1963): 281–283.

6.	The form of Grünzug Süd can be seen in relationship to Aldo van Eyck's protostructuralist projects, though Ungers was much more interested in achieving formal complexity by absorbing and reinterpreting the spaces of the existing city than in relying on behavioral patterns, as van Eyck's schemes did. See Dirk van den Heuvel, "Grünzug Süd Competition, Cologne Zollstock 1962–1965," in Dirk van den Heuvel and Max Risselada, eds., *Team 10, 1953–81: In Search of a Utopia of the Present* (Rotterdam: NAi Publishers, 2005), 154–155.

7.	There are numerous publications on Grünzug Süd. The most detailed analysis is in Oswald Mathias Ungers, "Erlauterungen zum Projekt Grünzug Süd in Koln," in O. M. Ungers, ed., *Team-X Treffen: 1965, Berlin* (Berlin: Technical University of

Berlin, 1966), 20–28. See also Wilfried Kuhn, "The City as Collection," in Andres Lepik, ed., *O. M. Ungers: Cosmos of Architecture* (Berlin: Hatje Cantz, 2006), 73.

8. This panel appears in Jürgen Pahl, "Betrachtungen über das Schaffen der Architekten O. M. Ungers," *Deutsche Bauzeitung* 71, no. 7 (July 1966): 580–581.

9. As recalled by Ungers in a conversation with Rem Koolhaas and Hans Ulrich Obrist. See Rem Koolhaas and Hans Ulrich Obrist, "An Interview with O. M. Ungers," *Log* 16 (Spring/Summer 2009): 75.

10. Ibid., 73.

11. Ibid., 76–77.

12. See the maps of Berlin illustrated in O. M. Ungers, ed., *Schnellbahn und Gebäude* (Berlin: Technical University of Berlin, 1967), 102–103.

13. See O. M. Ungers, ed., *Werkehrsband Spree* (Berlin: Technical University of Berlin, 1965–1966).

14. The project was for the area of Preussen Park and was executed by diploma student Ulrike Bangerter. See O. M. Ungers, ed., *Wohnen am Park* (Berlin: Technical University of Berlin, 1967), no page number.

15. See O. M. Ungers, ed., *Brandwande* (Berlin: Technical University of Berlin, 1971).

16. Koolhaas and Obrist, "Interview with O. M. Ungers," 63.

17. See Rem Koolhaas, "Fieldtrip, (A)A Memoir," in Rem Koolhaas and Bruce Mau, *S, M, L, XL* (New York: Monacelli Press, 1995), 570–578.

18. Ibid.

19. It is interesting to note the similarity between the subjects depicted in the photographs of the Berlin Wall that Koolhaas used to illustrate his memoir and those in Ungers's photographs of Grünzug Süd.

20. Grünzug Süd can be considered the first project to deliberately use a "systematic idealization" of the most banal features of the site. This attitude can be compared with Team 10's reality-as-found discussion (an attitude promoted by Peter and Alison Smithson), but Ungers's appropriation of the real went much further than Team 10's reformist approach, and toward a radical celebration of the least innocent attributes of the city.

21. Exodus was first published in *Casabella* in 1972. It was entered in the magazine's competition for "The City as a Meaningful Environment." For a complete illustration of the project, see Rem Koolhaas and Elia Zenghelis, "Exodus: or the Volun-

tary Prisoners of Architecture," in Martin van Schaik and Otaker Mácel, eds., *Exit Utopia: Architectural Provocations 1956–1976* (Munich: Prestel, 2005), 80–85.

22. Elia Zenghelis, lecture at the Berlage Institute, Rotterdam, April 3, 2004.

23. See Liselotte Ungers and Oswald Mathias Ungers, *Kommunen in der Neuen Welt, 1740–1971* (Cologne: Kiepenheuer & Witsch, 1972).

24. Oswald Mathias Ungers, "Le comuni del Nuovo Mondo," *Lotus* 8 (1970).

25. Oswald Mathias Ungers, ed., *Die Wiener Superblocks* (Berlin: Technical University of Berlin, 1969).

26. Koolhaas and Obrist, "Interview with O. M. Ungers," 81.

27. Colin Rowe and Fred Koetter, *Collage City* (Cambridge, Mass.: MIT Press, 1978).

28. Ibid., 105–107.

29. See Koolhaas and Obrist, "Interview with O. M. Ungers," 87. See also O. M. Ungers and Stefan Vieths, *Oswald Mathias Ungers: The Dialectic City* (Milan: Skira, 1997).

30. For a detailed explanation of the project, see *Lotus* 11 (1976): 21–27.

31. In the *Lotus* presentation, Koolhaas is not listed among the collaborators for Tiergarten Viertel, but Ungers's 1985 monograph names the Dutch architect as a collaborator. See Heinrich Klotz, ed., *O. M. Ungers 1951–1984: Bauten und Projekte* (Braunschweig and Wiesbaden: Vieweg, 1985), 254.

32. Peter Smithson and Alison Margaret Smithson, *Without Rhetoric: An Architectural Aesthetic* (Cambridge, Mass.: MIT Press, 1974).

33. Peter Smithson presented the part of the book devoted to Mies at Ungers's seminar. See Alison Smithson and Peter Smithson, *Mies van der Rohe* (Berlin: Technical University of Berlin).

34. For a detailed explanation of Ungers's project for Berlin-Lichterfelde, see *Lotus* 11 (1976): 28–72.

35. The barcode scheme is very similar to the strips OMA would propose in their La Villette Park competition entry in Paris ten years later.

36. As stated by Elia Zenghelis in a conversation with the author.

37. A few years after he met Rowe at Cornell, Koolhaas described his disappointment with the British theorist and historian: "Colin Rowe's modernism was completely stripped from its social programme, the social for him being the height of ridiculousness. In his book *Collage City*, there is a very revealing phrase: 'In this way we can enjoy the aesthetic of utopia without suffering from the annoyance of the political utopia.' It was the first time I was confronted with this tendency,

typically Anglo-Saxon, which later became more and more dominant." Patrice Goulet, "Interview with Rem Koolhaas," *Architecture d'Aujourd'hui*, no. 38 (April 1985), my translation.

38. Rem Koolhaas, *Delirious New York: A Retroactive Manifesto for Manhattan* (New York: Monacelli Press, 1994; first published by Oxford University Press, 1978).

39. Koolhaas uses this expression in "The City of the Captive Globe," in *Delirious New York*, 296.

40. In a short interview in Andy Warhol's magazine *Interview*, published at the release of *Delirious New York*, Koolhaas said that the Waldorf-Astoria was his model of living. See *Interview* (February 1979): 65.

41. Oswald Mathias Ungers, ed., *Berlin 1995: Planungsmodell für eine Fünfmillionenstadt in übergang zu den Siebziger Jahren* (Berlin: Technical University of Berlin, 1969).

42. These projects were published in the appendix of *Delirious New York*.

43. Rem Koolhaas, "Bigness," in *S, M, L, XL*, 495.

44. Oswald Mathias Ungers, "Planning Criteria," *Lotus* 11 (1976): 13.

45. Koolhaas, *Delirious New York*, 300.

46. Ibid., 302.

47. On the history of the concept of population, see Andrea Cavalletti, *La città biopolitica* (Milan: Mondadori, 2003). See also Michel Foucault, *Security, Territory, Population: Lectures at the Collège de France*, trans. Arnold I. Davidson, ed. Michel Senellart, François Ewald, and Alessandro Fontana (London: Palgrave Macmillan, 2007).

48. Cavalletti, *La città biopolitica*, 45–66.

49. Oswald Mathias Ungers et al., "Cities within the City: Proposal for the Sommer Akademie for Berlin," *Lotus* 19 (1978): 82.

50. Oswald Mathias Ungers, "Berlin as a Green Archipelago," *Lotus* 19 (1978): 45.

51. Rem Koolhaas, "Imagining Nothingness," in *S, M, L, XL*, 199–202. First published in *Architecture d'Aujourd'hui*, no. 238 (April 1985): 67.

INDEX

Krier, Léon, 178
Krier, Rob, 178

Laugier, Marc-Antoine, 162
Laws of the Indies, 8
Le Corbusier, 13–14, 25, 34, 48, 94
    City for Three Million Inhabitants,
        13–14
    Villa Savoye, 48
    Villa Stein, 48
Ledoux, Claude-Nicolas, 162
Lee, Pamela, 16
Le Muet, Pierre, 155–156
Lenné, Peter Joseph, 192, 224
Leo X (pope), 93
Leonidov, Ivan, 197, 224
Ligorio, Pirro, 64, 93–94, 95, 131,
    135, 137
Limbourg Brothers, 89
Lissitzky, El, 23
Livy (Titus Livius), 104
London, 105, 194, 197, 198
Louis XII (king of France), 62
Louis XIV (king of France), 105, 150,
    155, 158

Malevich, Kazimir, 23, 220
Mansart, François, 153
Mansart, Jules Hardouin-, 155
Marin, Louis, 109
Marx, Karl, 21
Mastrigli, Gabriele, 233n28
Maximilian I (emperor), 62
Mazarin, Jules, 168
Meda, Luca, 147
Mertins, Detlef, 36
Meyer, Heinrich, 29
Meyer-Christian, Wolf, 213, 214
Michelangelo Buonarroti, 13
Michelozzo di Bartolommeo, 119

Mies van der Rohe, Ludwig, xi, 23,
    34–44, 206, 209
    New National Gallery, 206
    Seagram Building, 34, 37, 38–39,
        42
    Toronto-Dominion Centre, 42, 43
Milan, 106
Mirabilia urbis Romae, 89, 93, 97, 98
Montalembert, Marc René de, 143
Morgan, William, 105
Morozzi, Massimo, 234n33

Nardini, Flaminio, 89
Neumeyer, Fritz, 36, 37
New York, 22–26, 37, 212–213,
    215–218, 219–222
Nicholas V (pope), 97, 100
Nicholas of Cusa, 25
Niemeyer, Oscar, 181
Nolli, Giovanni Battista, 89, 91, 106,
    115–116, 129, 131, 134, 137,
    138, 205
    Nuova pianta di Roma, 89, 106–115,
        116, 129, 137, 138, 139

Ockman, Joan, 236n55
Oechslin, Werner, 34
Office for Metropolitan Architecture
    (OMA), 180, 212–222
Ogilby, John, 105
Ovaska, Arthur, 177, 179
Overbeke, Bonaventura van, 89, 90

Palladio, Andrea, xii, 47–83, 109,
    119, 169, 172
    Basilica (Palazzo della Ragione),
        53–55, 56, 58, 59, 81
    Palazzo Chiericati, 56, 57, 58,
        59, 81
    Palazzo Civena, 49, 81